SIMON ARMITAGE

Walking Home

faber and faber

First published in 2012
by Faber and Faber Ltd
Bloomsbury House
74–77 Great Russell Street
London WC1B 3DA
This paperback edition first published in 2013

Typeset by RefineCatch Limited, Bungay, Suffolk
Printed and bound by CPI Group (UK) Ltd, Croydon, CR0 4YY

A CIP record for this book
is available from the British Library

Map © Eleanor Crow, 2012

ISBN 978–0–571–24989–3

2 4 6 8 10 9 7 5 3

Walking Home

Simon Armitage was born in West Yorkshire and is Professor of Poetry at the University of Sheffield. A recipient of numerous prizes and awards, he has published ten collections of poetry, including *Selected Poems* (2001), *Seeing Stars* (2010), his acclaimed translation of *Sir Gawain and the Green Knight* (2007) and more recently *The Death of King Arthur* (2012). A broadcaster and presenter, he writes extensively for television and radio, and is the author of two novels as well as bestselling memoir *All Points North*. In 2010 he received the CBE for services to poetry.

Further praise for *Walking Home*:

'Armitage has always been a wonderfully fluent writer, able to riff on almost any subject in either prose or poetry . . . The result is a homage to an oddly old-fashioned Britain, full of glorious eccentrics and hearts of gold, but vividly believable for all that.' *Financial Times*

'Huge Northumberland skies of mist and rain, moorland views, and clagging mud are all conjured up with astonishing clarity for the vicarious walker, sitting all nice and warm on the sofa.'
Independent on Sunday

'A charming book. There is a great deal of humour and keen observation in these pages and it is great fun to read about the highs and lows of Armitage's odyssey.' *Herald*

'This book is an enchanting read and moves Simon Armitage one step closer to the deserved accolade of "National Treasure".'
Walk magazine

'It's a book as likeable as the poet himself, funny, curious and tenderly observed.' *Country Life*

Map of the Pennine Way from Kirk Yetholm to Edale

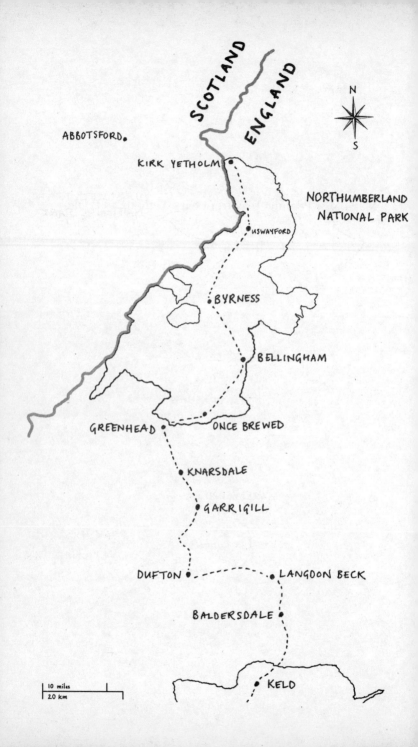

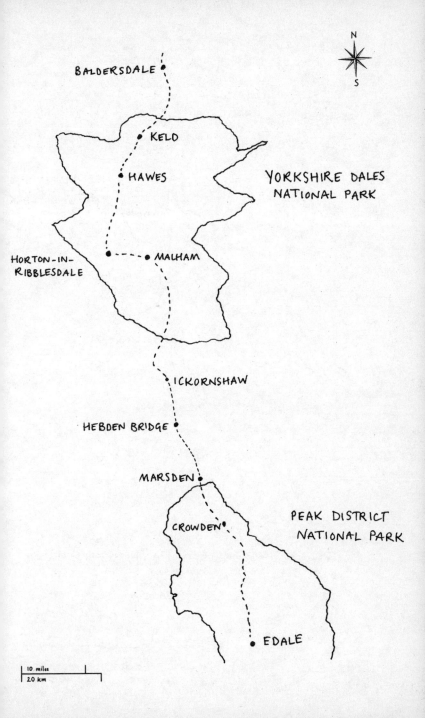

A Preamble

In the West Yorkshire village of Marsden where I was born and grew up, a peculiar phenomenon took place every year. Starting round about May, usually in the late evenings, foreign creatures in big leather boots and mud-splattered over-trousers began descending from the moor to the south. They carried on their backs the carapaces of huge rucksacks and, from a distance, silhouetted on the horizon, they looked like astronauts. Up close, they smelt of dubbin, Kendal Mint Cake and sweat. And having just completed the first and arguably most daunting section of the Pennine Way, they wore on their faces a variety of expressions.

When I was a child this regular arrival of hikers was a source of curiosity and entertainment. Sometimes they were looking for the now defunct Youth Hostel, a former Co-op with about a dozen beds and a pool table, which also operated as a hang-out for bored local teenagers. But more often they were looking for somewhere to pitch their tent. In the absence of any campsite, this was usually the football field, or somebody's garden, or, on one occasion, the roundabout at the top of Fall Lane. A couple of lads from East Kilbride liked Marsden so much they dropped their plan to hike north and camped at the back of the allotments for the whole summer, occasionally opening the flaps to emit great wafts of pungent smoke, to put their empty cider bottles out and to allow some of the village girls in. One old boy who knocked at my parents' house in desperate need of water still sends a Christmas card thirty years later.

The village welcomed these walkers; they were a good source of passing trade and to a certain extent put Marsden on the map. And without doubt, the walkers welcomed Marsden. Having set off from the starting post opposite the Old Nag's Head Inn in Edale, they would have covered a distance of about twenty-seven miles. That's a hard day's walk even through pleasant meadows or along a gentle towpath, but the first leg of the Pennine Way is a grim yomp across the aptly named Dark Peak, incorporating, just to emphasise the point, the equally aptly named Bleaklow and Black Hill. As kids, we roamed around the moors looking for adventures. But we always knew that beyond the immediate horizon, even beyond Saddleworth Moor which Myra Hindley and Ian Brady had turned into a macabre children's cemetery, there was a more foreboding and forbidden place. Looking up towards those moors from Manchester in the west or Sheffield in the south, it's difficult to understand: they seem little more than swollen uplands, humped rather than jagged, broad rather than high. But people go there and don't come back. Even on a clear day they form a bewildering and disorienting landscape, without feature or vista, like walking on a moon made largely of black mud. In the thick, clammy mist, which can descend in minutes, it is a nightmare. The Moorland Rescue team, friends of my dad, would sometimes come into the pub at night celebrating pulling a hiker out of a bog or finding some shivering wretch before nightfall. On other occasions a more sombre mood hung about them, and they sat quietly with their drinks and their thoughts. For those hikers arriving in Marsden after crossing the Dark Peak, the looks on their faces said it all. They had encountered something up there they hadn't anticipated, and the evidence wasn't just in their peat-clogged boots and their sodden coats. It was in their eyes. For many, the village of Marsden was not only the first stop along the Pennine Way, it was also the last.

*

The Pennine Way is about 256 miles long – no one seems to be able to put a precise figure on it – beginning in Edale in Derbyshire and ending in Kirk Yetholm, just the other side of the Scottish border. Britain's first official long-distance trail, it was formally opened in 1965, though hiker and journalist Tom Stephenson initially proposed the walk in a *Daily Herald* article published in 1935. Born out of the 'right to roam' movement, public disquiet after the great depression and the subsequent mass trespass on Kinder Scout in 1932, it was, in its conception, as much a political statement as a leisure activity, and no doubt there are members of the landed gentry with double-barrelled surnames and similarly barrelled shotguns who would still like to ban the common people from wandering across certain tracts of open moorland, especially during the month of August. According to the literature, many thousands of people hike some stretch of the Way each year, but of those who attempt the whole thing, only a fraction succeed. While taking in some of the most beautiful scenery in the country, it also passes through some of the bleakest. High above the tree-line, beyond even the hardiest sheep, some of the longer, lonelier sections represent a substantial challenge not just to the body but to the spirit. Indeed, if much of the literature is to be believed, the Pennine Way is more of an endurance test or an assault course than a walk, and not something for a feeble-minded, faint-hearted tenderfoot.

*

In the summer of 2010 I decided to walk the Pennine Way. I wanted to write a book about the North, one that could observe and describe the land and its people, and one that could encompass elements of memoir as well as saying something about my life as a poet. I identified the Pennine Way as the perfect platform: a kind of gantry running down the backbone of the country offering countless possibilities for perspectives and encounters, with every leg of the journey a new territory and a new chapter. But I decided to approach it in two unconventional ways. Firstly, I decided to walk from north to south. This might not seem like such a revolutionary act; a walk is a walk – can it really matter which is the beginning and which is the end? And yet the majority of people who complete the Pennine Way start in Derbyshire and breast the finishing line in Scotland. The theory, it seems, is to keep the sun, wind and rain at your back rather than walking for three weeks with the unpredictable and unhelpful meteorological elements of the British summer full in the face. Accordingly, all of the guide books are written in that direction. But as a poet, I'm naturally contrary. If most writers are writing prose, then mostly I'm writing something else. Poetry, by definition, is an alternative, and an obstinate one at that. It often refuses to reach the right-hand margin or even the bottom of the page. Prose fills a space, like a liquid poured in from the top, but poetry *occupies* it, arrays itself in formation, sets up camp and refuses to budge. It is a dissenting and wilful art form, and most of its practitioners are signed-up members of the awkward squad. So against all the prevailing advice, against the prevailing weather, and against much of the prevailing signage, I undertook to walk the Pennine Way in the 'wrong' direction. Walking south also made sense because it meant I'd be walking home. From what I'd read about the Way, almost every section of it offered multiple opportunities and numerous excuses to give up rather than carry on. I was going to need a consistent reason to keep going, and the humiliation of failing to arrive in the village where I was born seemed like the perfect incentive.

Secondly, and even more optimistically, I announced publicly that I would attempt the walk as a kind of modern-day troubadour, giving poetry readings at every stop, bartering and trading my way down country, offering only poetry as payment. Early in the year, I put the following page on my website.

The Pennine Way – Can You Help?

Hello. In July 2010 I'm walking the Pennine Way. It's usually walked from south to north but I'm attempting it the other way round, because that way it will be downhill all the way, right? I'm doing the walk as a poet. Wherever I stop for the night I'm going to give a reading, for which there will be no charge, but at the end of the evening I'll pass a hat around and people can give me what they think I'm worth. I want to see if I can pay my way from start to finish on the proceeds of my poetry alone. So, it's basically 256 miles of begging.

If you live on or near one of the recognised stopping points on the Pennine Way and would be willing to host or organise a reading for me, be it in a room in a pub, a village hall, a church, a library, a school, a barn, or even in your living room, do get in touch. If you can throw in B&B and a packed lunch, sherpa my gear along to the next stop, point me in the right direction the next day or even want to walk that leg of the journey with me, so much the better. I'm pretty well house-trained and know at least three moderately funny anecdotes.

Here's the schedule, outlining where I'll be and when, blisters permitting:

Thursday 8th July: Kirk Yetholm to Uswayford
Friday 9th July: Uswayford to Byrness
Saturday 10th July: Byrness to Bellingham
Sunday 11th July: Bellingham to Once Brewed (No
    reading – World Cup Final!)
Monday 12th July: Once Brewed to Greenhead
Tuesday 13th July: Greenhead to Knarsdale
Wednesday 14th July: Knarsdale to Garrigill
Thursday 15th July: Garrigill to Dufton
Friday 16th July: Dufton to Langdon Beck
Saturday 17th July: Langdon Beck to Baldersdale
Sunday 18th July: Baldersdale to Keld
Monday 19th July: Keld to Hawes
Tuesday 20th July: Hawes to Horton-in-Ribblesdale
    (Reading in Grasmere)
Wednesday 21st July: Horton-in-Ribblesdale to Malham

Thursday 22nd July: Malham to Ickornshaw
Friday 23rd July: Ickornshaw to Hebden Bridge
Saturday 24th July: Hebden Bridge to Marsden
Sunday 25th July: Marsden to Crowden
Monday 26th July: Crowden to Edale

And even if you can't offer a reading, if you see a weather-beaten poet coming over the horizon early next summer, do say hello. Many thanks.
SA

A fortnight before I set off I traced out the route and the reading venues with a pink highlighter pen, and couldn't find enough room in the house to lay out the nine required Ordnance Survey maps end to end. As a geography graduate who once dreamed of becoming a cartographer, I pride myself on a certain amount of navigational ability. But seeing the walk sprawled out in front of me, like some great long stair-carpet, the enormity and ridiculousness of the task started to dawn on me. Or to hit me, rather, as a series of bullet points, fired from close range.

- It's a long way.
- It's not a straight line.
- Some of the maps have very little in the middle of them apart from spot-heights and the names of hills.
- The only maps I've looked at for the last ten years are A–Z street maps, and not many of them either since the advent of the SatNav. Will I be able to cope without an electronically voiced Sally or Bruce telling me to go straight ahead at the roundabout?

- These maps are not handy and useful like road atlases, but wide, spineless and unwieldy sheets. It's hard enough trying to open them, let alone fold them back up again. What will that be like in the wind?
- Or the rain?
- For three weeks I will be reading these maps upside down.

I had, in fact, walked one section of the Pennine Way before. Or attempted it. In 1987, three of us took a train to Edale, being quietly confident of arriving back in Marsden for opening time. We were young, fit, and in good spirits as we walked west along the sunken lane from Grindsbrook Booth, crossed the old packhorse bridge and climbed the steep, rocky path known as Jacob's Ladder. It was a clear day. Or at least for an hour or so it was. Then it got dark, and cold, and the wind picked up. We were probably only two or three miles onto the moor, but we'd already entered that perplexing and mystifying lunar landscape, and we had gone astray. The night before, a man in the pub had assured us that it was impossible to get lost on the Pennine Way because 'it's basically like the M1 up there'. That man, it transpired, hadn't actually been on the Pennine Way and hadn't been on the M1 either. We stumbled around for a while, hoping to pick up the path, which had been right there beneath our feet only a minute ago then had vanished. We sat down on a stone to take an early lunch, but we'd eaten our sandwiches on the train. It started to get brighter, but that's because it was hailing, zillions of white, small-bore ice-balls stinging our faces and hands, making the ground and the air all the same colour. The map came out of the rucksack, got wet, and in the ensuing argument over who should take charge, was ripped into several soggy pieces. One of us thought we should find a stream and follow it downhill. Someone else said that was a bad idea and would lead us head first over a rock face or waterfall. Another suggestion was to stay put until we were rescued, which was voted on and passed, but after a minute or so of sitting in the silence and the chilly air and the frosty atmosphere, that began to feel like a very dispiriting option, and anyway, not one of us had thought to tell anyone where we were going. Finally we decided that the only thing to do, other than die, was to keep following the same compass direction until we came to a road. Manchester was on one side and Sheffield was on the other, it was just a case of holding our nerve and keeping to the same course. When we eventually stumbled off the hillside onto some minor road above Hayfield, we were only a few miles from our starting point, and Marsden felt a long way off, over impossible and impassable terrain.

*

Can I actually walk the Pennine Way? I have contemplated this question many times over the preceding months, and the truthful answer is this: I don't know. I'm forty-seven, I weigh twelve stone and twelve pounds, and when I look in the mirror, I see a reasonably fit, relatively healthy person. And from my father I have inherited a stubborn streak. Some people have interpreted this as 'ambition', but it isn't, it's just a pig-headed refusal to give up or accept failure, particularly when the chances of success are microscopically small or when defeat would be a far easier and more dignified option. On the other hand, I have an unspecified lower back problem that incapacitates me a couple of times a year, and although I wouldn't describe my lifestyle as sedentary exactly, it's certainly true that on certain days my legs do very little other than dangle under a desk or propel me from the multi-storey car park to the ticket office at Wakefield Westgate railway station. And from my mother I have inherited 'small lungs', apparently. I don't know if this has ever been clinically measured, but our poor capacity for storing and processing oxygen is family lore, and from an early age I was warned never to dream of being crowned King of the Mountains in the Tour de France or to take up a career as a pearl diver. In terms of training, I've done a bit of stretching and a bit of swimming, plus a few hours on a primitive cycling machine in my mother-in-law's back bedroom. I've also moved house. Only a couple of miles down the road, but hand-balling dozens of cubic metres of boxes containing thousands of books must count as some kind of physical conditioning. And I've been to Glastonbury, the original intention being to test my boots in the mud, though Glastonbury 2010 turned out to be a bit of a scorcher, so all I know is that my size ten GTX Mammuts are 100 per cent resistant to both dust and cider. 'I've done a lot of mental preparation,' I tell people, when they ask, and have reasoned with myself that I will undergo most of the physical training en route, preparing for day two by walking on day one, and so on and so forth. What could possibly go wrong?

Other people also seem to be in two minds about my chances of success. When I confide to a friend that I rate my odds as no more than fifty–fifty, he says, 'I admire your optimism.' And when, during the week before I set off, I ask my wife if she truly believes I can do it, she folds her arms, leans against the wall, looks at the floor, and says, 'Simon, I'm very worried about you.' Which I take to be a less-than-wholehearted *yes*. Or an indication that she considers me to be in the grip of a midlife crisis, needing to prove my youthfulness and manliness by hiking an insane distance every day for the next three weeks without a break, then at night, when I should be recuperating, giving public readings. Couldn't I just cut to the chase and buy a Harley Davidson or grow a ponytail instead? We're having this conversation in the kitchen. I'm getting my 'kit' together, and I've just come back from the garage with a purple and pink rucksack, hers, which has been hanging on a rusty nail for as long as I can remember and is a little bit moth-eaten. With her 'very worried about you' comment still hovering in the air, and possibly as a way of holding faulty equipment responsible for my imminent failure, I shake the dust and cobwebs from the rucksack and say, 'Do you think this is up to the job?'

'Well, it got me to Everest base camp without any problems,' she says, then goes outside to build a wall.

So, no pressure there, then.

A day or two later, I walk over to my parents' house, about eight miles away across the moor, to give the rucksack a trial run, and find that it doesn't really have all the necessary pouches and flaps to accommodate the complex paraphernalia carried by the contemporary hiker. My mum goes upstairs and pulls her own rucksack out of the airing cupboard, a big blue one with badges sewn on the front denoting her long-distance walking conquests. The fact that she completed the Pennine Way when she was fifty (carrying all her pack and with two dodgy knees, not to mention the small lungs) is just another reason why I MUST NOT FAIL. I remember going into the spare room before she set off, and seeing all her luggage laid out on the bed, including dozens of T-shirts compressed into a small dense block, and several weeks' worth of underwear which she had somehow managed to vacuum-pack into a couple of freezer bags, next to a travel-size packet of Fairy Snow. As well as the rucksack, she also gives me her Platypus, a soft, plastic water holder which sits in the side pocket of the rucksack and supplies liquid to the mouth via a tube, and I quickly try to suppress the Freudian implications of being lent such a teat-operated demand-feeding device by my mum.

My dad, who has been remarkably silent on the whole subject of me walking the Pennine Way, is sitting in the armchair watching *Cash in the Attic*, and is now ready to lend his opinion.

'Looks heavy, that bag,' he says.

'It's just a day bag,' I say. 'Everything else is going in a suitcase.'

'Give it here, let's have a feel.'

As if his arm is one of those spring-loaded hooks for weighing record-breaking carp at the side of a pond, he picks up the rucksack, then announces: 'Twenty-five pounds. Too heavy. You'll have to strip it down a bit.'

Like a naughty schoolboy turning out his pockets in front of the headmaster, I start emptying out the bag. When I packed it, I genuinely thought I'd included the minimum amount of gear for the maximum number of eventualities, but in front of my dad, everything now seems lavish and embarrassing, as if he's caught me with lipstick and mascara. So the camera gets a shake of the head, as does the notebook, the glucose tablets and the torch. Neither is he impressed with the GPS unit or the spare batteries or the packet of plasters, though the twelve-blade penknife does elicit a nod of approval. The last object in the bag, and one that takes up quite a lot of room, is a waterproof raincoat. Dismissing one of the fundamental tenets of hill-walking and demonstrating a complete lack of respect for the notoriously changeable Pennine weather he says, 'You don't need a coat.'

''Course I need a coat.'

'Nah,' he says.

'So what do I do when it rains?'

'Just take a bin bag,' he says. 'Cut a hole in the top and stick your head through,' he adds, before turning back to the television. For several days afterwards, I find myself thinking of the moment on *Look North* when I'm dragged from a ditch on some god-forsaken upland, wearing a refuse sack. Or wondering why my father would prefer it if I made my triumphant entry into my home village of Marsden, or perhaps more pertinently *his* village, dressed as rubbish.

Home to Abbotsford

Wednesday 7 July

On the morning of my departure, some kind well-wisher called James has emailed to point out that due to the centripetal forces induced by the rotation of the planet, the Earth actually bulges towards the equator, making the equator further from the centre of the Earth than the two poles, meaning that any journey from north to south in the northern hemisphere is not downhill, as I have commented on my website, but a climb. Thank you, James. And so it is with a heavy heart, a heavy rucksack, an even heavier suitcase and the laws of the universe stacked against me that I post the keys back through the letterbox and set off down the road. I have in my pocket enough money to get me to Scotland by public transport, and not a penny more. I am going for broke: from now on it's poetry or bust.

*

'I suppose I'll always be looked upon as the axe man, but it was surgery, not mad chopping.' So said Dr Richard 'Axe Man' Beeching when publishing his *The Reshaping of British Railways* report in March 1963, two months before I was born. I've only ever seen one photograph of Dr Beeching; in it he is wearing an Oliver Hardy moustache over his lip, a rather smug smile, and is sitting on a train – an irony that couldn't possibly have escaped him. Many said that Beeching's drastic cuts to the nation's rail network were short-sighted, which I agree with. On the other hand, it could be that his faulty vision actually saved the Penistone Line, a single-track route so insignificant and overgrown that it was probably overlooked rather than spared. To this day, I even wonder if the authorities are aware of its existence, or if it might be one of those operations staffed entirely by volunteers and enthusiasts, or even by ghosts. My local station isn't so much neglected as abandoned, even by vandals, and is a station only in the sense that it has a name and trains stop there, albeit not very often. Whatever the reason for its survival, it means I can catch a train pretty much at the bottom of the garden, even if the conductor can't supply me with a one-way ticket to Berwick-upon-Tweed. 'Change in Huddersfield then pay again,' he advises. Then he looks at my boots and my rucksack, and adds: 'Good luck.' I presume from this comment that he's seen something about my walk in the local paper, and taking his remark as a comic reference to Richard Attenborough's calamitous blunder in *The Great Escape*, I reply, '*Danke schoen.*' I see then from his expression that he has no idea why this English-speaking hiker should suddenly be spouting phrasebook German, and he moves off down the carriage in search of less complicated fares.

Huddersfield isn't a difficult town to leave. There are obviously a great many things I love about the place, because I've lived here all of my life and will probably die here as well, which has to be the biggest compliment anyone can pay their home town. But is it too much to ask for a little reciprocity every now and again, or that as admirers we shouldn't be required to work so very hard to justify our affection? On grey days like these, the view from the eastward-moving train is the organic architecture of an endless chemical plant with its elaborate and convoluted pipe-work set against the background of a dark and dirty hill. Leeds Road, in front of it, is a strip-mall of franchises and dealerships, and if the canal isn't actually clinically dead it's doing a very good impression of something no longer alive. The Galpharm Stadium is visually interesting, although its name is so ugly that even the most devoted Town fan rarely enunciates it, and the other two obvious landmarks are the red-and-black slab of the B&Q Superstore and the rocket-like chimney of the local incinerator. Huddersfield, I'm not running away, but just for a few weeks will you let me go?

The train is packed. It's odd to be a walker among so many workers, to put my rucksack on the luggage rack next to briefcases and umbrellas, and to see my big clomping boots lined up under the table next to pairs of shiny brogues and colourful high heels. But in some ways it reminds me why I'm making this journey, because thinking back, I was built for the outdoors. I had a childhood of moors and woods, of tree-houses and tents, of dens and camps. I went from the football field to the tennis court to the cricket pitch and rarely went home in between. I was a kite-flyer and a bike-rider. I stalked the undergrowth with an air-rifle. And I skimmed stones across the reservoirs, of which Marsden has dozens, as if the village had an inherent fear of dehydration which manifested itself in a mania for collecting and storing water, until every depression was flooded, every valley dammed, and every raindrop caught. The moor was wrung for its supply, brooks and becks were tapped and siphoned, rivers decanted into dye-pans and dams by the mill, and 'catch-waters' were dug out along the contours of the hills, like drip-trays a couple of yards wide and several miles long, drawing off every last droplet of moisture. Along with the railway and the canal it made the area a vast theme park of tunnels and bridges and shafts and tracks, an immeasurable, unsupervised playground. I imagined when I was younger that I'd spend my days and earn my living outside, and when I swapped social work for poetry, part of the idea was to get out of the office and into the wider world again, to rejoin the adventure. But the sediment has built up. The stodginess of routine has set in. So even if I'm writing about the Sahara or the Antarctic I'm usually doing it in a chair, in a room, behind double glazing. The Pennine Way is about getting OUT THERE again. It's about taking the air and clearing my head.

The commuters disembark at Leeds. I fall asleep against the window, wake up to see York Minster go past, then Sutton Bank with the Kilburn White Horse floating in the landscape. Then Durham Cathedral. The next time I look up it's towards sand dunes, the sea, then Holy Island and the superstructure of Lindisfarne Monastery, beached by a low tide. Familiarity dissolves with distance.

*

Al picks me up from the station. I've met him twice before, at a couple of Hogmanay parties about a decade ago. On each occasion we were both less than sober or we were hungover, but he'd spotted my SOS on the website, and recognises me on the platform, and we drive for an hour or so through the Scottish Borders, from one neat and tidy town to the next, across low, stone-built bridges and alongside wide, shallow rivers. I don't know this part of the world at all. It seems very orderly, very picturesque, and very empty. I once tutored a residential poetry course in a big farmhouse somewhere hereabouts. The lady of the house was generous and welcoming, but her husband didn't seem completely comfortable with the idea of poets poking around his yard and lounging on his settees, and made it his business to drive past the sitting-room window every five minutes on his mini-tractor while we were scrutinising some delicate piece of versification. Was that just down the road or a hundred miles away? The place names are familiar, but that's because when I see them I hear the voice of rugby union commentator Bill McLaren, saying, 'They'll be dancing on the streets of Hawick/Melrose/Galashiels tonight,' after some tousle-haired dairyman- cum-prop-forward had galloped half the length of the field and touched the ball down under the English posts.

With Al's wife Judith we eat posh fish and chips in a gastropub in Selkirk, then it's off to Abbotsford. Abbotsford isn't the start of the Pennine Way, but it is the home of Sir Walter Scott, and venue for the first reading. Al tours me around the formal gardens, past the glasshouse, in and out of the sculpted hedgerows, then across a mown stretch of meadow to the bank of the Tweed. There's a marquee on the lawn; Abbotsford might be the spiritual home of one of Scotland's most famous sons, but like most historic sites and country piles it needs money and plenty of it, so for the right price you can get hitched here. I imagine the amplified strains of Whitney Houston or Tom Jones bouncing off the ornate masonry and echoing around the walled vegetable patch. In the house itself, we pass through a corridor decorated with Scott's collection of weaponry: swords, pistols, daggers, pikes, armour, plus the heads, horns and hides of many an unfortunate beast. Scott was unable to fulfil his ambitions as a military man because of a bout of polio when he was two which left him lame, but what he lacked in physical ability he obviously made up for in arms and artillery. Like Lord Byron with his club foot, he clearly wasn't embarrassed by the concept of over-compensation. The galleried study is marvellous, a wonder, and somewhere in the background I can hear Al pointing out the wax seals, the quill pen, the lavish handwriting and the handsome spectacles . . . But I'm not looking. Or listening. My mind's drifting. I'm thinking of the 256 miles and nineteen consecutive poetry readings stretching away to the south. I've made a big song and dance about this venture, talked about it on the telly and the radio, written pieces for the papers, roped in dozens and dozens of volunteers to cart my bag and lay on events and give up their beds. The whole project is based on the kindness of strangers, the entire itinerary held together by nothing more than a loosely connected chain of names and addresses and telephone numbers of people I've never met and who don't know me from Adam. But the weakest link in that chain, I now realise, standing here among the trappings and trophies of Sir Walter Scott's epic deeds and dazzling accomplishments, is me. What the fuck was I thinking? Failure seems unavoidable, with humiliation and shame the inevitable consequence.

But it's too late now, because the glasses from the champagne reception are being collected, and I'm being introduced, in the library, with a white marble bust of Scott staring down on me in judgement from the mantelpiece. In front of the great bay window, I explain what I'm doing here, and how I'm leaving a hat by the door – all contributions welcome. In fact I've decided to leave a sock instead, still a clean one at this stage, on the basis that it allows for more discretion when making a donation and even offers the possibility of taking something out rather than putting something in, should the reading offend. Then I launch into the first poem, one hand on my book, one hand on a display case containing a lock of Bonnie Prince Charlie's hair and Rob Roy's sporran. Towards the end, several people in the audience seem moved to tears, covering their eyes with their hands and bowing their heads. One woman takes a handkerchief out of her bag and lifts it to her face. But it's just the sun, setting directly behind me, streaming into the library, blazing around my head and behind my back, reducing me to flames.

*

I'm staying with Catherine and John in Kirk Yetholm. Or is it Town Yetholm? Or perhaps even Thirlestane? In the twilight, through the car window, one place seems to bleed seamlessly into the next, but as every villager knows, at the local level these kinds of distinction are fundamental. To the Town Yetholmer, Kirk Yetholm may as well be Timbuktu, an elsewhere, a place unlike their own, where they do things differently. A cork comes out of a bottle of wine and Catherine takes an order for my breakfast and packed lunch. A conversation gets under way around the kitchen table on the relative merits of the treasure-trove system, John's land having recently yielded up some historic artefact. I tell them a story I heard on the news, about a man with a metal detector who unearthed an exquisite Anglo-Saxon torc. He knew he had to hand it in to the authorities, but just for one night he gave the golden necklace to his wife, and she wore it for dinner. I embroider the tale, so she enters the candlelit kitchen in a flowing white gown and satin slippers, and he carves and serves the specially prepared dish of a wren inside a quail inside a guinea fowl inside a turkey inside a swan. Then they toast their good fortune with a goblet of mead, royalty for a day, king and queen of their own little world.

In the guest bedroom there's no signal to call home, not even if I stand on a chair or lean out of the window. I get under the sheets, drift off dreaming about buried treasure and hoards of gold, then wake up realising I haven't counted the takings from the reading. With the rest of the house asleep, I empty the sock onto the bed as quietly as I can. It's a scene I wouldn't want to explain, the awakened householder bursting in with his gun and his dog to discover the avaricious and perverted northerner standing there in his underpants and T-shirt above an eiderdown glittering with money. I count the coins into piles. There are notes as well, some bearing the face of Sir Walter Scott. In my notebook I write, 'Abbotsford: Attendance, 72. Takings, £167.77.' Then with the money scooped back into a Tesco's carrier bag I go back to sleep, and wake up five hours later when the alarm goes off, not sure where I am and with a two-pence piece stuck to my bare thigh.

The Border hotel
end of the Pennine Way

Kirk Yetholm to Uswayford

15 MILES

OS Explorer OL16 East Sheet

Thursday 8 July

The threshold of the Border Hotel, standing at one side of Kirk Yetholm's village green, is thought of by many as the finishing line of the Pennine Way, with the hotel bar as a sort of winners' enclosure. Some of the guide books and Pennine Way publications are a little bit snotty about Kirk Yetholm itself, but this is largely to caution the exhausted though euphoric walker who rolls up expecting to be met with congratulations and praise. Because there will be no open-armed welcome, no ticker-tape strewn from bedroom windows, no fly-past by the Red Arrows, and outside stern and vigorously applied Scottish licensing hours, not even a drink. So despite the fact that the Pennine Way is its biggest claim to fame, it's best to assume that Kirk Yetholm won't give a flying toss about yet another bedraggled hiker staggering into town after an epic walk. No matter how long it has taken or how painful the journey, the Pennine Way is an individual accomplishment, a form of private satisfaction, and any sense of triumph should be limited to a strictly personal level.

There is, however, a book to be signed, some sort of ledger or roll of honour, but the hotel is closed and the curtains are drawn. I knock several times, until I hear bolts sliding and the sound of a big key in an old lock. A woman in a dressing gown and with sleep in her eyes squints at me through the half-opened door.

'I'm setting off on the Pennine Way and I'd like to sign the book,' I say.

'You sign it when you finish,' she says, then closes the door.

*

There are ten of us and a dog setting off this morning. Most of them are still laughing at my rejection as we huddle for a group photograph next to the Pennine Way signpost, then next to the Pennine Way illustrated notice board, the dotted red line of the route meandering between etchings of curlews and waterfalls, with two idealised ramblers in shorts and basin cuts consulting a map. Rendered in that style and reduced to that scale, it looks like child's play. An afternoon stroll. A walk in the park.

There's a gentle climb along a metalled road for a mile or so, then the Way splits, a 'High Level Route' continuing east, and a 'Low Level Route' forking south. Taking 'low' as a measure not only of altitude but also of experience and confidence, we head south. Outside a farmstead, a lorry container emblazoned with the red, white and gold of Tunnock's Caramel Wafer Biscuits is being utilised as a stable, and an angelic, blue-eyed, rosy-cheeked boy radiates his enthusiasm and appetite for the *Tons of Taste in a Tunnock's*. The cart track along the valley bottom eventually becomes a worn strip of grass as it leaves the last cattle-grid and farmyard and heads into the hills. But before it does, a car pulls up and the poet Katrina Porteous gets out. She's brought cakes, and a great many of them. I'm only a couple of miles in and I'm stuffing myself with gingerbread and Victoria sponge. 'A cakewalk,' I tell everyone, rather pleased

with the pun. Everything feels good. It's a clear day, my boots are comfortable, and a couple of horses are nodding agreeably by an electric fence. Four of the party say their goodbyes and turn back. We pass a dilapidated farmhouse on the right, where a stoat hops about on a cracked lintel, unperturbed by our presence. In my part of the world, a walk in the hills is nearly always a painstaking trudge over ankle-breaking tussock-grass or through saturated peat bogs, but these Borders foothills are smooth and firm underfoot, appearing from a distance to be lawned and mown, like the emerald baize pastures of Romantic paintings. It won't last, but for now it's a green and pleasant land that our feet walk upon.

Katrina hasn't just brought cakes, she has brought a memory. A number of years ago she came here with a man, and walked up through the tumbledown settlements of Old Halterburnhead and Piper's Faulds, and stopped at a gate, between the peaks of Black Hag to the left and the Curr to the right. They sat down on the grass together – there was no one else around. Like all good poets, she knows that silence and empty space are just as important as the words. Then the man asked her a question. She doesn't say what it was; an invitation or proposal of some kind I imagine, life-changing, dramatic, exhilarating, impossible. Her heart said yes, but her mouth said no. To which the man replied, 'You have said NO to the universe,' carved the word NO into the gatepost, then took up a stone and cast it away into the valley. As we pass by the gate, she hangs back, hearing the question again maybe, maybe looking for the carved word, perhaps this time saying yes. A couple of years before he died, Ted Hughes suggested I read a book by Thomas Charles Lethbridge, the Cambridge-educated archaeologist and keeper of the Anglo-Saxon antiquities at Cambridge's Archaeological Museum, a man whose scholarly reputation wavered as his interest in 'alternative realities' grew. Lethbridge became a scientific experimenter, investigating aspects of the occult such as psychokinesis, divination and even ghosts. *The Power of the Pendulum* puts forward a theory of dowsing by means of a pendulum. In its practical application it becomes a kind of magical metal detector, the pendulum responding to metal buried in the ground, the length of the pendulum relating directly to the type of metal. He also suggested that recollections can inhabit or cling to places, and that objects can become infused with the sentiment of an experience. So we shouldn't be surprised when we feel the atmosphere of a battlefield or graveyard, or sense the emotional charge of a chair or a knife. Or a gateway, such as the one Katrina stands at, in the distance now, triggering memories by touching the wall or ruffling the grass with her boot, or just disturbing the air with her presence.

Tim and Claire are also lagging behind, either because they're birdwatchers or because they're newlyweds. They catch up at the border. Not just any border, but the border of Scotland and England, and it's somewhat disappointing that the dividing line between the two nations, across which so much blood has been spilt and so much animosity exchanged, should be little more than a wooden ladder. We all take photographs and I try to summon up the gravitas of the occasion by standing with a foot on each side. But T. C. Lethbridge would have been disappointed, because I feel nothing except for an inflated sense of progress, i.e. it's only day one and already I've walked into my own country. The dry-stone wall running south-south-east makes a semi-dignified effort as a national boundary, the air-blasted, lichen-covered grey stones holding out against the weather and the gradient. Just. But eventually the wall downgrades to an apologetic post-and-wire fence, through which anything and anyone might pass. We scramble up to the top of the Schil and find shelter from the wind behind a rocky outcrop. There's more cake, which Claire cuts with her pocket knife.

'It's not going to be full of toenail clippings, is it?' I ask, when she passes me a slice.

'No, this is the blade I use for dissecting birds,' she says, with a mouthful of crumbs.

Through the binoculars we watch the skies, but focus eventually on the more disturbing sight of police vehicles,

sniffer dogs and armed marksmen at the bottom end of College Valley. Five days ago, Raoul Moat, recently released from Durham Prison, went on the rampage with a gun, wounding his ex-girlfriend, killing her new partner, and blinding a police officer by firing at him twice from just a few feet away, sparking what is being described as 'Britain's biggest ever manhunt'. Moat was last spotted near the pretty Northumberland town of Rothbury, the 'Capital of Coquetdale', usually a picture postcard of tea shops and hanging baskets, but today a hotbed of police activity and a media circus. There isn't a room to be had in the town, apparently, nor a stottie left in the bakery. Even the Met have been called in, though it's hard to imagine anywhere less metropolitan than these environs; park rangers and big-game hunters would have been a more useful conscription. Moat is said to be armed and dangerous, not to be approached under any circumstances. It seems unlikely to me that as a fugitive he would choose a well-worn section of a national trail during the summer holidays, but who am I to second-guess the moods and actions of a wanted man. Some grisly, tragic outcome feels inevitable. The binoculars go back in their case and we move on.

It tries to rain but it can't. Cows lumber freely across the lower slopes and through high bracken, like big slow balloons, with no obvious sign of ownership or restriction. The view in every direction is delicious: a solar system of summits, majestic but benign hills overlaid with lush grass and the odd rectangle of planted conifer. And somewhat incongruously, in the far distance to the east, the sea. The higher ground, usually a morass of liquefied peat and standing water, is bone dry, courtesy of an unusually rain-free spring and hot early summer, meaning a stubbed toe is more likely than a wet sock. We make good time, springing and bouncing over the dehydrated turf, marching across the stone slabs, promenading along the two or three wooden boardwalks. Like long, low pontoon bridges spanning vanished watercourses, the planks on these boarded sections have turned bright silver through years of bleaching by stinging rain, penetrating frost, scalding wind, and, this year, relentless sunlight. In the Mountain Range Hut we have our second lunch and say hello to three men with chapped lips and sunburnt faces who are walking the other way and are almost home and dry. One writes operas. The second is retired. The third man, Nick, says, 'Are you Simon Armitage?' He's read about my walk in the *Huddersfield Examiner*, compounding my suspicion that wherever you

1st April
to
31st May
except for
access

travel in the universe, someone from the Huddersfield diaspora will have got there first. Either we are born to travel, or we can't bear to stop at home. Once, on a beach in Spain, I inadvertently tuned a shortwave radio to the commentary on a Huddersfield Town semi-final play-off, and ten minutes later there were eight Town fans standing around me, four of them in replica shirts. One of my party, Steve Westwood, then confirms my theory by admitting that he lives at the bottom of my road. As National Trail Officer, Steve has to walk the Pennine Way several times a year, so is acting as guide today. On his advice we don't detour up the highest point in the Cheviots, the unimaginatively named and apparently unrewarding Cheviot, which is more of a swelling than a peak, but stick to the path as it dog-legs to the south-west, and a few hours later we're standing at the top of Clennell Street, an ancient drove road or 'escape route'. Many walkers, especially those on the last leg, take a deep breath and complete the twenty-seven miles from Byrness to Kirk Yetholm in one day. Less intrepid souls, like myself, need to break the journey in half, and Clennell Street is the only realistic option for getting off the hills for the night. The rest of the group say goodbye and go north to rendezvous with a Land Rover parked at Cocklawfoot, and I go south with Mel from Northumberland National Park. The forestry track drops down to Uswayford, pronounced *Oozyford*, which appears to be not much more than a house and a wooden chalet, no longer offering B&B. The plan is to keep walking until someone called Gareth meets us in his car. But I'm knackered, and the cinder path is hard on the feet. So I suggest we sit down at the top of Murder Cleugh (where IN 1610 ROBERT LUMSDEN

KILLED ISABELLA SUDDEN according to a commemorative stone), and enjoy the view, which is at its most
agreeable when a powerful estate car comes haring up the
valley, rattling over the cattle-grids and kicking up dust.

Gareth is the landlord of the Rose and Thistle Inn in
Alwinton, my lodgings for the night and venue for the
reading, being the nearest alternative to pitching a tent and
reciting poetry to a few sheep. He offers me a pint, but until
I've broken the back of this walk I'm on the wagon. Al has
kindly delivered my suitcase, which has already acquired
the nickname of the Tombstone. Gareth tried to porter it
earlier in the day, then quite rightly decided to leave it for
me to carry upstairs to the room. It's not easy, packing for
three weeks of walking in unpredictable weather and three
weeks of poetry readings to unpredictable audiences, but
even so, the case is absurdly heavy, the kind of inert and
uncooperative weight I associate in my mind with a dead
body. I eat all the individually wrapped shortbread biscuits
in the wicker basket by the mini-kettle, then go for a stroll
around Alwinton. It doesn't take long. A dozen or so houses,
if that. A bridge. A river with picnic tables on the bank.
Pinned on the inside of the wooden bus shelter between
adverts for a barn dance in Hepple, quiz night at the Star
Inn in Harbottle and details for Margaret's Yoga Class,
there's a poster for a poetry reading. Under my mug-shot
are the words, 'Free – no need to book.' The phone box next
to the bus shelter doesn't take actual money, only credit
cards. I don't think I've used a payphone since calling Dial-
a-Disc in 1979. When I eventually get through to home,
having followed half a dozen voice-prompts and entered
several hundred numbers, it's the answering machine.

I read in the lounge bar. Gareth has turned the jukebox off but can't silence the fruit machine, the intermittent hum of beer coolers, the clack of pool balls or the chatter of locals in the snug. Poetry has this effect on background noise – start reading, and everything else becomes amplified. In the presence of the spoken word, the scrape of knife against plate or the opening of a packet of salted peanuts are nuclear explosions. At one point, a crying child in a Cinderella dress wanders across my line of sight. Raoul Moat's face keeps flashing up on the muted TV screen. Two waitresses sashay between the stools and tables with dirty plates and vinegar bottles, oblivious to any element of performance, although when the younger one does finally realise what I'm doing she 'ducks' beneath the poem as she passes in front of me with a Cumberland sausage. Eventually, a kind of quietness settles over the proceedings. It never reaches that level of concentration where even the trees outside seem to come to the window to listen, but enough to hope that a few words or even sentences have hit home. Afterwards, a man at the bar, who insisted on sitting behind my back in the furthest corner of the pub, says, 'You were all right but you need to speak up.' I spread the map out on the pool table, and study tomorrow's route with Sarah from South Shields, who has offered to sherpa the Tombstone to Byrness in the morning. Rather than driving home tonight, she is sleeping in a tent outside, just a few miles upstream from where an armed killer is said to be lurking. In the room I tip out the sock and make a note of the numbers. 'Attendance: 22 [about ten of which had probably just come out for a quiet meal], takings: £31.55.' Down at the toe end of the sock I feel the encouraging rustle of paper. But it's something far less crude than money. It's a poem by Katrina, called, 'The Answer.'

I go to the phone box again but there's no light bulb inside and outside it's pitch black. It's only ten o'clock but there's nothing to do so I turn in. It's a twin room. I take the bed next to the wall, and the Tombstone takes the one by the door.

Uswayford to Byrness

OS Explorer OL16 East Sheet/West

Friday 9 July

A softly spoken ranger in an impressively equipped Land Rover drives me back up to the trail. He talks with what is probably some finely nuanced accent peculiar to just a few square miles of rural Northumberland, but to me he sounds pure Geordie. Because there's a killer on the loose his team have been advised to work in pairs, and he tells me to take care before swinging the vehicle around then accelerating back down the forestry track, stone chippings spitting and popping under the chunky tyres. Fugitive gunmen aside, I've been looking forward to today, to walking on my own. It's blowy and fresh, clear and bright, and the slabbed causeway forms a very obvious and inviting path, a yellow brick road of sorts, stretching from cairn to cairn, from one peak to the next, in pretty much a straight line. An hour later, I'm lost.

A few weeks before I set off I made a list. Two lists, in fact:

Not Afraid Of	Afraid Of
Solitude	Loneliness
Bulls	Bullocks
Farmers	Farmers' Dogs
Rain	Fog
Darkness	Blackness

[35]

Criticism	Humiliation
Strangers	Weirdos
Fatigue	Blisters
Distance	Time
Getting Stuck In	Getting Lost

And now, after just a few miles of solo journeying, it looks as though I've sleepwalked my way across that no-man's land between the left- and right-hand columns, and pretty soon will have to face down at least two of those fears, and possibly four. It all goes wrong somewhere near Windy Gyle, or Split the Deil as it's also called. Somehow, I have got it into my head that today's journey is a long slow curve in a vaguely south-westerly direction, without any particular deviation or divergence. I'm also guilty of appalling, amateurish complacency. Yesterday, I'd simply followed in the footsteps of people who know the Pennine Way from back to front, so the map and the compass had stayed in the bottom of my rucksack all day. This morning, I've been striding forth at the same cocky pace and with the same casual attitude, imagining that I would be ushered and guided by the kindness and companionship of the land itself. But the land doesn't care, not one jot, which is why it has delivered me halfway down a boggy moor along a path which is becoming narrower and fainter with every step, and which eventually fragments into half a dozen vague and wispy sheep-trails, like the frayed end of a rope. The GPS unit, also at the bottom of the rucksack, underneath two rounds of beef sandwiches and three slices of treacle flapjack, was only bought as a toy really, or as a last-gasp, never-to-be-used safety measure, like a maroon or cyanide tablet. I spread the great picnic blanket of the map on the wiry heather, power up the device and watch as it blinks and meditates, scanning the heavens before locking on to a signal. Then through a combination of the most sophisticated satellite technology and the ancient, incontrovertible laws of trigonometry, it pinpoints my position on the planet to an accuracy of, at worst, ten metres. But of course I know better. I'm utterly convinced that I should be heading towards a plantation about three miles directly ahead, and towards the very inviting valley beyond it, so off I go, for another mile or so, by which time there is no path whatsoever, and no stile or gate in the very stern-looking fence that stands in my way and stretches off as far as the eye can see both to the left and to the right. The hills which only twenty-four hours ago seemed so noble and benevolent are now mountains, intimidating and unforgiving, looming rather than rolling, multiplying in size and number, becoming angrier under darkening skies. Standing among them, the only person in a vast and empty landscape, I feel both utterly insignificant and intensely scrutinised at the same time. I think about home. I think about Raoul Thomas Moat. True, I'm only lost in the sense that I have gone wrong, and I could easily walk back the way I came. But then what? Even from Clennell Street it's another seven or eight miles to Alwinton, with all the inevitable ignominy and indignity of having failed at the first hurdle. Plus the Tombstone is now in Byrness, and so is tonight's reading. The sound and sight of rain landing on the open map could easily be mistaken for falling teardrops. And yet, and for reasons that I can't explain, I continue to prefer my own judgement over that of the compass or the GPS, both of which are obviously

BROKEN and USELESS. Clearly, all I need to do is to match the topography with the cartography, but infuriatingly the hilltops do not announce their names in big letters, and the valleys between and beneath are similarly unidentifiable. As if wrangling the map in the increasing wind wasn't enough, I'm also wrestling with a pair of elasticated over-trousers and a waterproof jacket, and my hat is being blown down the hill on the other side of the fence. And now running seems like a good idea. Running after the hat. Running after the map. Running to the top of the hill to see what lies beyond it (more hills, as it turns out), running to the bottom of the hill to pick up a stream (there isn't one), and finally running all the way back to Windy Gyle, where sitting down is now a better idea than running, because I'm out of breath and upset. The only place to get out of the wind and rain is the lee side of Russell's Cairn, which I'd ignored earlier on the basis that if you've seen one cairn you've seen them all, and it's only while sheltering beneath it that I spot another path, the right path, scored through the thin topsoil into the bedrock, dipping away to the right then rising again across the valley, looping from one peak to the next into the distance. A minute later, when I find a marker post with the initials PW on it, I don't just want to hug it, I want to marry it and have its children.

*

There's a Mountain Refuge Shelter after Lamb Hill, like an oversized garden shed or an ironically positioned beach hut, with a little veranda, a small gate across the door to prevent infiltration by sheep, and a grandstand view of the unfolding

emptiness. I'm damp, chilly, shaken up and in a bit of a sulk, so I don't even open the visitors' book to read the comments, let alone write a poem in it, which had been my ambition at the beginning of the day. I don't eat either, even though it's the only place for lunch on a ridge-walk like this, the peaks being too cold and windy, the troughs being too miserable and wet. I just want to push on. It's illogical, but I feel as if I'm late and need to make up for lost time. The path jogs sharply to the west then turns south. I know this because I have the map out now, in its waterproof case. It hangs from my neck on a length of string, occasionally catching the breeze and slapping me in the face. Then there's a tramp through pathless doldrums to the west of Wedder Hill, a mossy and boggy heath where the air becomes still and silence descends, until I feel almost becalmed. Again, it's satisfying to find a signpost at the far end, after refusing to be sidetracked by the trails left by quad bikes delivering cattle feed, or those arcane paths through the rushes and grass made by mountain hares. After delivering the Tombstone, Sarah has walked up from Byrness to reel me in, and finds me eating a banana on a wooden bridge, being buzzed by a squadron of horseflies who hadn't tasted human flesh until ten minutes ago and couldn't believe their good fortune when my hot red face and ripe bare skin came hoving out of the distance.

We pass a sign pointing to nowhere with the word *Heartstoe* on it, and a less ambiguous notice saying DO NOT TOUCH ANY MILITARY DEBRIS, IT MAY EXPLODE AND KILL YOU. Just after noon I'd watched several dark green vehicles moving along a sinister, unmapped road in a far valley, and all day the noiselessness of the hills has been punctuated by the pounding of exploding ordnance, with plumes of white smoke rising from the southern horizon, vibrant and distinct against the grey clouds. Persisting with the military theme, I'd been expecting some kind of impressive stronghold or towering citadel at Chew Green, but despite the Roman Fort's five-star review in many of the guide books I don't even know that I've walked across the tumbled remains and scattered earthworks until it's too late, and I'm not going back. The massif of the Cheviots is behind me now, and in the distance lies a flatter, gentler, calmer prospect. I have walked across an entire *range*, and although the Cheviots are not the Alps and I am *sans* elephants, for a moment or so, I am Hannibal. Thereafter, the descent into Byrness is impatient in its directness, the path rapidly losing altitude as it plummets through chest-high bracken, descends a rocky escarpment and pushes aside the ordered ranks of spruce and pine which stand in its way as it makes for the metalled landing strip of the A68.

*

The village of Byrness isn't much more than a few houses at the side of the road, though marked prominently on the map are a phone box, a church, a hotel and the local sewage works, so it could be argued that not only are life's basic necessities adequately covered, a few luxuries are also catered for. The community developed as workers' accommodation at the time when the forests and reservoirs of Kielder were being planted and built, and has somehow managed to maintain an existence long after its original purpose. Cars and lorries hammer along the main road next to the tidy, mown square criss-crossed by footpaths, which is giving a passable impersonation of a village green. White terrace-cottages frame the square on three sides, and if Byrness could be thought of as a Monopoly board, then Joyce and Colin are clearly in the lead, because as far as I can tell they seem to own most of it. Their unpretentiously named Forest View Walkers' Accommodation does what it says on the tin. It's also run with the sort of regimented orderliness usually associated with the armed forces, and perhaps because she was anticipating the arrival of a wounded soul from one of hiking's frontlines, Joyce has billeted me in the disabled annexe, a kind of cottage hospital without a nurse. She leads me up the concrete ramp and points out the newspaper (last week's *Observer*) where I can park my boots, and the 'wet room' where I can shower and sit on the toilet at the same time, should I be so inclined. The bedroom is accessed by a sliding door, wide enough to admit a wheelchair, and wide enough therefore to admit the Tombstone, which looks like it has been sinking into the mattress for most of the day, its ponderous weight causing the eiderdown to rise up around it. I lie next to it for a while in the fug of my own fumes and the stickiness of my cold sweat, contemplating the significance of a disabled suite in a hostel whose only clients are walkers on Britain's most difficult trail. Because even with a fully functioning set of limbs and organs I'm already knackered, and it's only day two.

Colin isn't much in evidence – I wonder if he's convalescing after manhandling the Tombstone through the house and hoisting it onto the bed. So when I'm feeling more human and have made myself presentable, it's Joyce who gives me the guided tour, although the number of notices on every door, cupboard and available surface mean that things are pretty self-explanatory. In fact there's so much signage that I have to wonder if Joyce and Colin also have their own printing company, or at least keep the nearest laminating business in handsome profit. 'No Dogs Beyond This Point.' 'No Boots In The Hostel.' 'Please Open The Window In The Morning To Ventilate The Bathroom.' Every room comes with its own set of instructions, warnings and forfeits, including one sign forbidding residents from drinking their own alcohol in either the grounds or the building, the penalty for flouting this law being instant eviction without refund. The communal kitchen is spotless, with a place for everything and everything in its place, and a plastic card saying exactly where that place is. Joyce has

achieved a Level 2 Award in Food Safety; I know this because the certificate is pinned on the notice board. In the fridge, every item carries a price tag, including Laughing Cow cheese at 15p per triangle and big-ticket items such as the 45p yoghurts. But the retailing highlight is the self-service arcade in a cupboard under the stairs, selling all manner of foodstuffs and sweets to entice the weary walker. Much of the stock is reminiscent of a bygone age, like the tins of chopped ham or oxtail soup, or the little jar of beef spread, and the whole display is both quaint and artful, comforting and disquieting at the same time; I could be looking at the back wall of a sixties corner shop in a museum of social history, or I could be in a Cork Street gallery being baffled by a Damien Hirst installation. Purchases are made via an honour system, and seeing me eyeing the gold ingot of a Crunchie bar, Joyce hands me a credit slip and a biro.

I'm shown the drying room where some serious-looking kiln-like machine is exuding fierce quantities of arid heat ('This Room Must Be Kept Closed At All Times'), then to the room where I'm to give the reading, a residents' lounge with four leather settees and a wood-burning stove.

'Perfect,' I say, meaning that it has a door that closes and no pool table.

'Well,' she says, 'it is Byrness.'

'Yes,' I say.

'Although someone who left this morning is coming back to hear you, and a man telephoned to say he's driving up from Bath and not to start without him.'

*

Nine people come to the reading. By which I mean the nine people sitting in the residents' lounge attend a poetry reading whether they like it or not. This includes a father-and-son team from Wales doing the Pennine Way in three stages, a woman from Kelso who was (of course) born in Huddersfield and knows my mother, and a truly magnificent wiry old boy from County Durham who has walked 230 miles in seven days carrying not much more than a pac-a-mac and a packet of mints. I'm thinking of the audience as small but international, though Joyce dismantles this notion by pointing out that her two German guests have stayed in the kitchen. Joyce doesn't attend the reading herself, even though I sense she would have liked to. Instead she hovers outside, popping in every now and again, taking orders for drinks and nibbles. Colin, I assume, is nursing his hernia or spellchecking signs in the office. After the poems, the conversation turns firstly to the dangers posed to walkers by horseflies, or 'clegs' as they are sometimes known, which can bite even through heavy fabric and are only dissuaded by Avon Skin So Soft, the repellent of choice not only with foresters and trawlermen but also with British troops in Iraq and Afghanistan, apparently. Then secondly to sheep ticks, those hook-mouthed bugs which hang around in bracken and ferns, whose one ambition in a short and lonely life is to bury their head deep into the soft tissue of any passing creature, hikers included. One person says they only occur in areas where there are deer, another that they can only be removed with a naked flame (though the proposer of this theory admits that on the one occasion when he attempted such a procedure he was left with both a sheep tick and a nasty burn), and a third person that the bodies can be removed by twisting, but this leaves the head of the creepy-crawly impaled in the flesh, which can then enter the bloodstream. A doctor in our midst pooh-poohs this notion, impressively pointing out that sheep ticks are an essentially subcutaneous infestation, and more easily removed when dead, when the insect no longer has the power to cling on with its teeth, though he will admit that a decapitated sheep tick can become septic if not extracted, and that a living tick can grow to the point where its legs can be seen wriggling about under the surface of the skin, and that Lyme disease can follow, followed by death.

Takings for the evening are £32.50 plus a betting pen. I fall asleep listening to the news on a transistor radio. Raoul Moat is now cornered on the banks of the River Coquet, caught in night-vision binoculars and the crosshairs of several police marksmen, and with his own gun nestled under his chin. His mother is reported as saying that he would be better off dead, a position, surely, from which there is no desire to return. To complete the picture, tragi-comedian Paul Gascoigne has travelled 'all the way from Newcastle to see Moaty' with a can of lager and a chicken dinner, to offer counselling and advice.

Byrness to Bellingham

15 MILES
OS Explorer OL16 West Sheet, OL42 West/East

Saturday 10 July

Because of her dedication to the cause, and for running a no-nonsense, shipshape operation, and for trusting that a poetry reading can take place in the middle of nowhere against all the odds, and for the packet of ham and Branston sandwiches wrapped in clingfilm with an extra chocolate biscuit on the side, I have become a big fan of Joyce. I give her a hug before I leave, then she straightens her hair and sets off into the dining room to clear the tables. The man from Bath turned out to be the poet Matt Bryden; with his girlfriend Camilla and their shaggy grey lurcher, Jess, they have made the valiant several-hundred-mile drive not just for the reading but for today's walk. They don't know how they will get back here tonight to pick up their car, but in a spirit of great optimism and talking like some dyed-in-the-wool countryman with a thousand years of experience under his belt, I tell them not to worry, something will turn up, someone will help out. 'It's like that in these parts.'

The trail strikes south-east out of Byrness, towards a campsite and over a little bridge, running parallel with the road and jinking either side of the River Rede, fresh and lively this morning after a downpour in the night. The sun makes fleeting appearances between the long, low clouds, illuminating the crowns of trees overhead, occasionally spearing through the branches and leaves and striking the ground at our feet. We walk on under the canopy, young beech and birch trees loaded with last night's rain, showering us as we brush past. Sometimes the river veers away, presenting a grassy bank in the open air – a good place to picnic or pitch a tent – then swings back into the woods, forcing the path to choose a route through sodden, knee-high sedges. It's easy and enjoyable, a classic English footpath meandering among broadleaf trees and summer flowers with the sound of running water never far away, the day full of promise and possibility, the legs willing, the mind eager and the flask still hot, and it is to be enjoyed while it lasts, because after just a couple of miles, at somewhere called Blakehopeburnhaugh, the Way kicks to the right. The new direction brings with it a new terrain, new weather (it's drizzling now) and a new map, most of it jade and emerald in colour, scored with the dead white veins of Forestry Commission tracks and inscribed with millions of tiny dark green Christmas trees – the OS insignia for a coniferous plantation.

During my childhood, holiday destinations seemed to be chosen more for their imagined ambience, or even their names, rather than for any specific leisure activity. 'We're going to Mull,' my dad would say. Or, 'This year, what about Devon?' One summer we went to Inveraray, where there was a hill at the back of the guest house and a loch in front, so for two weeks we went up and down the hill in the rain, or played in the water, and as far as I remember it wasn't a problem, although spotting the big black fin of a basking shark on the first day made us nervous swimmers. Sometime in the early seventies we went on a camping trip to Northumberland. There were some monuments here and there, apparently, which would be enough to keep us occupied for a fortnight. But the only memory I have is of midges, unlimited in number, each one ferocious and insatiable. We arrived in the evening and had to wear plastic bags over our heads while we put the tent up. The midges also provided a kind of curfew, ensuring that as daylight began to fade, everyone on the campsite would retreat under canvas or lock themselves in the car. Ten years later, having had such a wonderful time, we decided to go back. Using the same dog-eared road atlas we drove to the same place, only to find that in the intervening years it had become submerged beneath many billions of gallons of water which formed the largest man-made reservoir in Britain, nestled within Europe's biggest man-made forest. As well as providing an infinite supply of liquid refreshment for the region's midge population, Kielder Water was built to service the heavy industries of England's north-east coast, but by the time the reservoir was opened those industries had all but disappeared. Some claim that Kielder is not only a white elephant but an environmental calamity, the monoculture of Sitka spruce and its lookalikes signalling the end of biodiversity and effectively carpeting over what was once a rare and treasured moorland habitat. Those with vested interests argue otherwise, that the forest provides sanctuary for endangered wildlife such as red squirrel and raptors, that it offers endless recreational facilities, and that the reservoir, in a warmer world with an uncertain meteorological future, is a well that never runs dry.

Monoculture possibly, monotonous without doubt. In fact it's plain old boring, slogging along the gravel access road with a drawn curtain of trees on either side. But after yesterday's escapade on the hills, boring means not getting lost, which is good. Today I like boring, because it gives me chance to take stock, catch my breath and my thoughts, and to think of the road as a kind of catwalk while I try out various combinations of rainwear and hats from my rucksack. I even begin writing a poem in my head, something I never do if I'm feeling rushed or stressed. I've also realised how important the map is; even on an apparently straightforward stretch like this, the road forks or the path sneaks off into the trees for half a mile or so without warning. It's important to keep checking, and in some ways, more essential to know where you've been than where you're heading. A sheepfold, a disused quarry, even a thin wire fence: tuning into this fine-scale cartography takes time and concentration, but being able to put a finger on the map and say with absolute confidence I AM HERE makes the air smell sweeter and the sandwiches taste fresher. We stop by a closed metal gate to eat, and the midges come swarming onto us, on our hands, in our hair, our ears, our mouth, up our noses. Keep walking and it's fine, but pause for a second and they materialise, the descendants of those midges that feasted and gorged on my bare legs when I was seven, and have inherited the taste. On we go. A forestry worker in some ginormous mechanical contraption lifts felled trees from one pile and drops them on another. It seems churlish of him not to return our wave, given that he probably won't see anyone else for another twelve hours, but maybe he doesn't notice us, in his glass cabin, under his hard hat and his ear defenders and several layers of Avon Skin So Soft. Maybe he just hates people, in which case, he's found the perfect employment. Jess trots alongside, uncomplaining and obedient, the ideal animal companion as far as I can tell, but a savage beast, according to Matt, when deer are around. In the water-meadows of Somerset this tame pet has suddenly become electrified at the sight or sound or more likely the smell of a roe deer, and several times has bolted off into the long grass and returned later with a claret-coloured face, a trail of blood leading to some beautiful wild creature four or five times its size with its throat ripped out. Sheep: not interested. A rabbit: take it or leave it. But once a deer enters the picture, this cute toy dog with its schoolgirl name and pretty collar becomes a killer. Becomes a wolf. Every now and then I look down or up or along one of the firebreaks, those mysterious, beckoning fairways cut into the forest, expecting to see deer, and on two or three occasions I'm not disappointed. But they dissolve in an instant into the brush and undergrowth. Ghostly, telepathic, clairvoyant beings; they knew we were coming long before we arrived, and know to disappear before the aerial of Jess's tail stiffens and points, and before her eyes turn red.

The trail leaves the forest as it climbs towards Brownrigg Head, following two parallel fences and six or seven partly submerged white marker stones. It's the first quagmire of the journey, impossibly wet and soggy, surface water up to a foot deep where there should be a path, meaning we have to tack off to the right looking for terra firma or hopscotch along the tussocks, a game that inevitably leads to sore ankles and wet boots. Down the steep pitch of Gorless Crag it's so sodden that one guide book actually suggests walking on the wall, except the wall has fallen down either through waterlogged foundations or by people using it as a bridge.

More deer in the wood to the west see us coming and dematerialise. Thinking that I'll vault across one particularly nasty-looking ditch, I realise I've left my walking poles back in the wood, having put them down to tie my bootlace then gone sprinting off before the midges could devour me.

'I thought you were walking better,' says Matt.

I loved those poles, for their aluminium lightness and their metallic blueness and their clever telescopic retracting and extending abilities, and not least because of the small fortune I paid for them. But all the love in the world won't make me go back over that swamp.

'They'll turn up,' Camilla says, trumping me with the same kind of optimism that could leave them stranded in Bellingham tonight.

A party of six, including two dogs, are coming towards us in single file as we're squelching up the opposite side of the valley. Having noticed my itinerary on the internet, William had been in touch with a vague and what I thought was an impossibly loose plan to intercept me somewhere on this stretch, but here he is, with his family and his picnic basket, right on cue. On the rump of Padon Hill, on a flat rock, we sit, eat, drink, talk. As far as I'm able to gather between gusts of wind, William is a London solicitor in the week, a Northumbrian farmer at the weekend, and a patron of the arts in his free time. The offices of Bloodaxe Books, my first publisher, are stabled in one of his estate buildings, which he points to, somewhere in the unknowable distance, with his index finger.

'So where is your farm?' I ask him.

'Here.'

'Where?'

With a sweep of the arm which seems to take in every square mile of land in every direction either side of the Pennine Way, he repeats his previous answer. 'Here.'

After the pit-stop, William and co. see us over the scrubby heather of Whitley Pike, direct us towards a stand of trees in the middle distance, then peel off. The wind rages and the rain lashes, but it's superficial, cosmetic rain – it doesn't mean it – and we're heading downhill, and for reasons that are probably all to do with biscuits and cake I'm feeling energetic, exhilarated and full of self-belief. As a demonstration of this newfound I'll-do-whatever-I-want confidence I get the camera out and take an arty photograph of a quad bike tyre being used as a feeding trough, and a few minutes later, decide to pee in the middle of the moor. Decide to piss in the wind, in fact, as if I'm so powerful I can even disprove a universally acknowledged truism. If there was a tide nearby I'd probably try to turn that back as well. Matt and Camilla are more tactful, making use of a roofless, tumbledown, brick-built outhouse, while Jess stands guard under the lintel.

Even though the setting isn't particularly dramatic, there's more surface variation here, certainly more than the uniform greenness of Kielder Forest and more also than the cover of bracken and grass thrown over the Cheviots. A patchwork rather than a blanket, to the point where the landscape closely resembles the map, or even becomes the map itself, making it possible to dead-reckon by distant features, such as Hareshaw House, where three big horses stand impassively in the front paddock, unimpressed by our presence, selectively blind and deaf as we scuttle past. A narrow B road abseils the arched back of a distant hill. To the left, the stony, terraced grandstand of Callerhues Crag becomes prominent then recedes. To the right, the Linn Plantation opens up beneath us before closing behind. Moor becomes heath, heath becomes meadow, meadow becomes field. A golf course on the other side of the valley seems absurdly manicured, conspicuous in its form and lurid in colour. We are returning from another world. Bellingham, pronounced Bellinjam, is tucked somewhere beneath the hill. My schedule, fished out of the rucksack, says I'm staying with someone called Dick, and this must be him, sitting on a stone bench with a cap on his head and his coat zipped right to the top, his hand coming forward to shake mine. As we walk down the lane towards the town we call in at the Heritage Centre to collect the Tombstone. Lovely Joyce dropped it there earlier, then Dick took one look at it or perhaps experienced some of its gravitational pull, and decided to leave it to me. So much for the epiphanic arrival: I scramble the last fifty yards dragging the embarrassingly enormous and embarrassingly turquoise suitcase up Dick's steep lane, its wheels screaming under the weight and gouging two deep ruts across a tended grassy verge.

*

These are the difficult hours. A new town, a new house. The back bedroom, decorated with photographs of children long since grown up and piles of books never to be read again. A towel on the bed. Someone else's bathroom. The arcane knowledge required to operate a temperamental shower, the leverage needed to give the toilet a proper flush, coming downstairs with wet hair to a family of strangers talking in accents and dialects other than your own. The desire to curl up in a ball and lock the door, the obligation to explain yourself, to engage in conversation, and to smile. Not that Dick is anything other than generous and kind, and it can't be much fun for him either, having a complete alien inhabiting his domain, witnessing his rituals, fiddling with his appliances. Dick's ex-daughter-in-law lays out what in our house is known as a Sunday tea: cold meats, quiche, rice salad, bread rolls, soup, a plate of tomatoes – a bit of everything to be eaten in no particular order. The older of Dick's grown-up grandsons is at university, the other is thinking of joining the police but doesn't know why, and I can't work out if Raoul Moat's confused and chaotic death a few miles downriver, with rumours of Taser wires and sniper rounds, has given him second thoughts or whetted his appetite.

The reading has all the ingredients of a fiasco, being outside, in a flapping marquee, between bouts of rain, midges and folk music. But it's a beautiful thing. A shepherd, unaccompanied and smelling of a pipe tobacco my dad used to smoke, stands up and sings a couple of traditional ballads. (By traditional I mean I can't understand a single word but it sounds heartfelt and authentic.) A guitarist and a squeezebox player make smutty jokes, sing saucy songs and poke fun at neighbouring towns. A young fiddler and flautist make an appearance, even though they're due to leave in the early hours of the morning for a musical adventure in some remote and exotic part of the world and still haven't packed. A woman plays the Northumberland pipes; from where I'm sitting, on a wall at the back, it looks like she's giving physiotherapy to a small marsupial wearing callipers and smoking a bong, but the sound is haunting and hypnotic, mournful and melodic at the same time, every note somehow harmonising with the low, droning purr. And I read my poems. Attendance: 76. Takings, a gratefully received £211.17. I've only been on the road three days but somehow I already seem to have several friends: Katrina is in the audience, and William of Bloodaxe and co., and a photographer I met on the way to Dick's house, and a guy from the mountain rescue team I bumped into yesterday, and a woman who tells me she played bass with one of my favourite bands, the Wedding Present.

'Wow. Which album?'

'Dunno. The silver one.'

'*Saturnalia*?'

'Might have been.'

'I love that album.'

'Yeah. I should listen to it.'

On the way to the pub afterwards for an abstemious lime and soda and to buy Dick a pint, I tell myself that this is what community is. People of all shape and stripe, pulling together, putting up a big white tent in a car park and doing their thing. Community is also Matt and Camilla getting a lift back to Byrness with the two German girls staying with Colin and Joyce. Then again, in the Black Bull, community is several dozen of the local yoof drinking premium-strength continental lager and singing karaoke, and in the Chinese takeaway, community is a handful of voluble Otterburn squaddies in uniform ordering chicken chow mein, and when these two groups crash into each other on the high street after closing time, as seems inevitable and almost obligatory on this highly charged Saturday night, that will be community as well.

'Sometimes I shout out in the night,' says Dick, as we're going up to bed. But if he does I don't hear him. I fall asleep thinking of my lost poles lying cold and alone in Kielder Forest, so ergonomically pleasing and so reassuringly expensive, but gone. I really loved those poles.

Bellingham to Once Brewed

14.5 MILES

OS Explorer OL42 East Sheet, OL43 East/West

Sunday 11 July

The weight of the Tombstone is not being helped, I realise, by the steady accumulation of lots of dosh, much of it in the form of pound coins. Unfortunately, I'm never within ten miles of a bank during opening hours, and there seems little prospect of off-loading the money until lower down the trail. I transfer the coins into a knotted T-shirt and push it towards the bottom of the case. Rolled into a fat wad, the notes go into a waterproof Tupperware box then into the rucksack. The other object adding to the mass is the year's supply of Mars Bars given to me by my wife the day before I set off. They're World Cup Mars Bars, branded with the England football strip, and following the Germany game in the Free State Stadium, Bloemfontein, very cheap. I've been scoffing as many as I can – this trip is going to be as tough on the teeth as it is on the feet – as well as offering them to fellow walkers, random hikers and even moorland animals, but as yet there is no obvious evidence of depletion, and a great number of them have morphed into a dense paving stone of chocolate and glucose somewhere between the layer of underpants and the rainwear stratum. Guide books are heavy as well. Instead of carrying them, I've been razoring out the relevant pages to take with me each day, slicing up books in my pyjamas, as if sitting up half the night in a stranger's boxroom counting used fivers wasn't furtive enough. But from now on I'm aiming to read and memorise, then just trust to the map.

By eight sharp I'm walking past Dick's recycling bin, overflowing with the damp, scrunched-up balls of newspaper I'd stuffed in my boots overnight, then down the steep path behind the leylandii hedge and alongside the site of last night's gig, where the marquee has been dismantled and the area forensically cleansed of any poetry-related activity. Bellingham-pronounced-Bellinjam is still dozing: condensation clings to the two police cars parked outside the stone-built station; a faulty light in the cashpoint machine flickers on and off; two old-fashioned petrol pumps straight out of an episode of *Heartbeat* stand like saluting sentries in the forecourt of a local garage. The path tries to hide round the back of the graveyard, but I find it, and stroll along the river, then past other features I remember from the guide books – the stone bridge, the campsite, the Forestry Commission District Office. I'm glad to be on my own today, to have a bit of a Laurie Lee moment, rising early, leaving the town while it's still in bed and heading into the wild blue yonder. A steep climb up Ealinghamrigg Common gets the knees pumping and the heart pounding, and now the breeze is picking up, a sharp, clean knife of air, the kind which pares away the layers of torpor and lethargy that build up around the spirit and the soul over the years. The wind increases as I rise through the contours, until at the top of the hill I turn west into the most tremendous surge of fresh air, a screaming and buffeting jetstream, and I take off my hat and undo my coat, letting it pummel my face and rip at my hair and hammer my chest. Directly in front, the most astonishingly vivid and perfectly symmetrical rainbow makes a glorious archway over a distant relay station, exactly where I'm heading, and for a moment or so I feel welcomed and blessed, invited by higher powers through this portal of colour and form designed for my benefit alone, forgetting temporarily that rainbows are the product not only of light but of water. So what the heavens are really announcing is rain, and ten minutes later, it's a gale.

I wrap up and press on. Past Shitlington Crags (an opportunity for a childish joke in better weather and better humour) and Shitlington Hall (ditto), a sprawling farm actually, where I have my first encounter with dogs. Five of them, collies, come bundling and bouncing across the yard, four of them all bark and no bite, the other one growling ominously around my heels, though when I spin around it

sits down, and from the milkiness in its eyes and the way it looks into some vacant space over my shoulder I think it might be blind. Much of the Pennine Way traverses private land, and today the trail seems determinedly invasive and assertive in its routing, passing continuously through gates, yards, crops, livestock, along cart-tracks, and close to buildings, windows and doors. Some land-owners appear to have accepted and allowed for its presence, guiding walkers across their property via careful landscaping or explicit notices, in stark contrast with a thankfully smaller group of mutterers, grumblers and saboteurs who obviously can't abide the daily procession of work-shy trespassers. The majority, though, seem ambivalent as to its existence, making no positive contribution to the upkeep of the trail but not actually hindering its progress. At Lowstead, a renovated cluster of buildings on the bank of Blacka Burn, the Way actually approaches the main house along its tarmacked drive, takes in two sides of the neatly mown lawn then winds through a rambling garden before vaulting a stile and heading off up the side of the valley, to the next farm, then the next, then the next. And somewhere between Leadgate and Horneystead, a fairground teddy bear used for target practice spews stuffing from its exit wounds, as does another teddy nailed to a tree trunk. A decapitated scarecrow in a blue boiler suit slumps forward in a deckchair facing the path, though I choose not to take it personally. Neither am I offended when a couple drinking tea in a hardwood conservatory refuse to return my smile; to me the moment might seem unique, but to them I'm just another idiot in the rain, and no doubt they've seen thousands of them. Pennine Way folklore tells of the route actually

running through a residential bathroom at one time. I'm a great believer in the right to roam, but not enough of an activist to insist on hiking past a homeowner's shower curtain or gatecrash some other confidential act of sanitation.

The wind keeps gusting and the rain keeps driving, and I keep thinking that the weather will 'blow itself out' – it's an expression I've heard – as if the same technique used to extinguish oil-well fires could be applied to meteorological conditions. But to the west more and more dark clouds keep on massing above the horizon. A small plantation comes and goes, and once out in the open again it occurs to me just how exceptionally empty and unpopulated this part of the world is. So far I've seen only eight other people, one of whom was filled with straw. Quite rightly we get anxious about the natural world being concreted over, and about loss of animal habitat and the unstoppable spread of the urban environment. Unarguably we have gone too far. But for those looking for rural seclusion or a place where they might go properly bonkers without anyone else either knowing or caring, then fear not, because a great many opportunities and possibilities still exist, especially in Northumberland.

I get whatever shelter I can under a pair of birch trees at the side of a single-track road and eat a soggy sandwich, then cross a field of rough grass towards a low, flat water-meadow, one of those unsung but transforming sections of the Pennine Way where one world hands over to the next, where half a dozen foxgloves and tall, flowering thistles are positioned like torches or flares either side of the track, which leads towards a high, shadowy entrance formed of larch, through which a planted wood is entered. Where, despite the man-made artificiality of it all, I suddenly feel comforted and assured. Stumps of old trees are footstools upholstered in velvety green moss. Pine resin is the first thing I've smelt for hours. Except at the very top where their tips bend and flex like fishing rods in some mad struggle, the evergreens absorb the bruising gusts and deafening surges of wind, so there's nothing but static and stable air at ground level where I walk. And somewhere above me, where their coats are thickest and fullest, the trees have absorbed all suggestion of rain, so down here it's dry and cushioned, every footfall received and relaunched by a thick mattress of spongy, brown needles. A form of twilight gathers under the canopy, a cloistered stillness, and sometimes the patterns of upright timbers form alleyways or avenues, heading off through the forest towards an open glade or sunlit grove. I imagine deer, furlongs away, ears tuned already to the clumsy juggernauts of my boots and the heavy industry of my breathing, safe in the knowledge that at any moment they can simply melt away. Then without warning the trees stand aside and a small wooden gate opens onto the wide, wind-blasted expanse of Haughton Common, and as I emerge into its tremendous emptiness, I'm surprised by how quickly my mood can change on this walk, how many reversals of spirit take place during the course of a day. Half an hour ago I was saturated and glum, chunnering to myself about the pointlessness of the whole project, dreaming up an excuse to quit. Then came the tranquillity and calm of the woods, and now this plain, this prairie of papery bleached grass, each blade like a palm cross, shaking and zithering in the air-storm. In fact the wind is so powerful and so absolutely and directly against me that I have to almost cycle into it, lifting my knees then pushing back against imaginary pedals, dropping into the lowest gear. And the further I climb the more adamant it gets in its opposition, as if a whole North Atlantic weather front has come bursting through the collapsed dam of Bellcrag Flow, pouring through the gap, so that any progress is progress upstream, against the flood, into the rapids, with boulders and logs of hard air piling into me and knocking me sideways. It should be torture, but it's exhilarating, ecstatic, a frenzied initiation or hysterical reacquaintance with the great outdoors. And I think: this is why I came, to stumble into the unexpected, to feel the world in its raw state. I open my mouth to shout MORE, but the force of air just rams the word back into my mouth and down my throat. Halfway up the hill there's a four-sided sheepfold housing a handful of stunted trees that appear to have endured this sort of thrashing and flaying for hundreds of years. Pilloried, they are, and lashed, twisted into knots and bent out of shape, yet in spite of the scorn and the punishment, or possibly because of it, they cling on, alive. I push past them, shouldering through the torrent of air, and notice now that my clothes and boots are completely dry, and see how the sun has rived open a gap in the sky, and that other cracks are opening up in the cloud base, and tears roll down my face, and not just because of the wind blasting against my eyes, or even the sudden light.

Kielder Forest comes to an end on a down-slope facing due south, and the path can be seen meandering onwards between Greenlee Lough to the right, sharp and cold-looking in that harsh, scrubbed brightness which often follows rain, and Broomlee Lough to the left, above a hump of moor. I crouch down under a wall to rummage around in the rucksack for a sandwich, but my hand can't penetrate further than the geological layer of Mars Bars about a third of the way down. A ruminating heifer peers over the wall to observe my lunch break. As the sky keeps clearing, I see what appears to be a thick, dark line in the distance, all the way across it, in fact, as if the horizon had been drawn by a child using a black crayon or a pencil. In ten minutes the mirage doesn't fade, but gets stronger and more vivid, the line now a definite feature, a bold and continuous edging or hem, like a stroke of heavy eyeliner where the sky meets the earth. It's not until I flip the map over and unfold it a couple of times that I realise I'm looking at the leading edge of the great Whin Sill, rearing up out of the ground in the north-east of England and baring its teeth at Scotland. And not just at that formidable volcanic extrusion, but at the famous barrier running along its crest, namely Hadrian's Wall. If the Great Wall of China can be seen from space then perhaps I shouldn't be so surprised that a comparable feat of engineering is visible from just four miles away, but even so, it's an unexpected and impressive vision.

*

Before I made this trip I read most of the available Pennine Way literature. All of it suggested that for reasons of weather this is a summer-only journey, but also advised that national holidays are best avoided due to the amount of 'traffic' on the Way, as if what should be a reflective and contemplative experience might be marred by the sheer number of walkers. One guide book and several websites put the number of people 'doing' the Pennine Way each year as high as a hundred thousand. But while it is true that I have only been going for four days, already I can say with a certain amount of confidence that such estimations are bullshit. Here I am, slap bang in the middle of the high season, and I am virtually ALONE. Admittedly most people walk south to north and many give up at some stage, making these northern reaches the quietest – only the die-hards and the oddballs get this far. Nevertheless, a drop-out rate of about 99.9 per cent would be required for the mathematics to make sense. On the first day I passed seven walkers, five on the second, none whatsoever on day three, and so far today only two. Up in the Cheviots, after getting lost, I was elated to finally clap eyes on another human being, a solitary walker in blue waterproofs about a mile off, heading my way. I rehearsed a few relieved lines of conversation, imagined a handshake perhaps, maybe even a celebratory swig from a hip flask and a bit of man-to-man backslapping. Eventually the distance between us shortened to a hundred yards, then ten, then just a few feet, at which point the stranger grunted an incomprehensible sound from somewhere under his rain hat, sidestepped me on the path and accelerated away up the other side of the valley. The Pennine Way might be the first, the mother-of-all, the Route 66 and the Trans-Siberian Railway of long-distance walks, but it is also an unglamorous slog among soggy, lonely moors, requiring endurance and resolve. As such, it faces stiff competition from those newer leisure trails rich in car parks, information centres, tea shops, gift shops and conveniences of all kinds, with celebrity-chef restaurants and four-star accommodation along the route, plus significant termini at each end, such as national borders or the sea. In comparison with those 'boutique' walks, the Pennine Way is forty days in the wilderness.

Except, that is, on Hadrian's Wall, where most of the above-mentioned facilities can be found, and which forms a substantial section of the increasingly popular (if unimaginatively entitled) Hadrian's Wall Path, stretching from the Solway Firth to the Tyne Estuary. As a consequence there are PEOPLE, thousands of them, either milling about on the milecastles for photographs, or picnicking at the viewpoints, or striding along the ramparts attended by children, grandparents and dogs. The Wall is a wonderful thing, quite breathtaking in its ambition and construction, and to walk beside it seeing England roll away smoothly to the south and Scotland rise and swell to the north is to *feel* its purposes and its implications rather than just understand them as history and archaeology. But among so many other human beings all of a sudden, I can't help feeling a little bit crowded, then even a mite superior, irritated by the presence of so many civilians and amateurs trespassing on my pilgrimage, staining the purity of my mission. So I don't bother with Housesteads Roman Fort, aka Vercovicium, a detour of only a few hundred yards, on the basis of it being a tourist attraction therefore inappropriate to my higher status. I can also see that it's swarming with school parties and day-trippers. Instead I get my head down and turn directly west, marching forth, looking up only now and again to acknowledge the view or to study the ultra-vivid lichen growing on the south side of the Wall, every blotch and bloom like a green country or green continent on the square grey map of each stone. The other thing I notice, on the far side of the wide valley running parallel to the Wall, is a white dot, travelling at great speed. I wonder at first if it's an optical problem on my part caused by so much exposure to the wind and the rain, a kind of Pennine snow blindness, or the hiker's equivalent of 'seeing stars' brought about by dehydration and exhaustion. But I rub my eyes and it's still there, still travelling at an implausible rate of knots, sometimes lengthening, sometimes shrinking to a small point of light, like an electron, I think, a scrap of pure white energy speeding across the ground like nothing I can understand or explain. As it draws level with me, perhaps half a mile distant, I realise it must be a dog, a single white dog, but no one around seems remotely interested in why a dog should be running hell-for-leather across the middle of nowhere, neither chasing or being chased. And now it seems to be made of liquid, so fluent over walls and across streams, morphing and transforming as it passes through fences and stiles. On it goes, until it dissolves altogether into the backdrop of hills. I scan the whole circumference of the horizon and the entire bowl of the valley for an anxious dog-owner or irate farmer following on tractor or quad bike, but there's no one at all, and now nothing to say that the creature even existed, just a mirage in the mind of a tired man whose daily exertions don't usually extend much further than daydreaming or reading a book.

*

Along here the path and the Wall coexist, so I'd have to work pretty hard to get lost. Turn left and I'd roll down the hill, turn right and I'd plunge down the cliff face into a quarry or pond, so the map is only needed to identify and name-check features and landmarks, such as Vindolanda Fort and the small settlement of Bardon Mill, then Haltwhistle beyond it, and the confluence point where the Allen meets the South Tyne, their direction of flow just enough to remind me I'm walking uphill. At Peel Crags a group of mean-looking cows are sulking and skulking by the gate, so I track up over the top of the rock face and emerge in the middle of some kind of fair or country show. Thirty or forty 4x4s and pick-ups of varying size and configuration have pulled up on the grassed area beyond the car park, plus umpteen vans and horseboxes with their tailgates down. Next to the coffee and cake stall a trestle table covered by a plastic awning displays several gleaming silver cups and engraved salvers. In areas penned off with plastic tape, men and women are standing with their dogs while a chap in a tweed suit and tweed hat looks into each animal's eyes and holds up their tails for inspection. The dogs in this section are lean and wiry lurchers or greyhounds, and give the impression of walking in high heels as they trip and totter around the site, gazing in fear or adoration into their owners' faces. Trusting entirely to stereotypes and presumptions, the owners themselves seem to come from the upper or lower tiers of society but there are no obvious representatives of the middle classes: a woman in a herringbone skirt, posh wellies (i.e. with a buckle on the side) and a Barbour jacket stands next to a man in shellsuit and trainers with prison tattoos on his neck and a roll-up in his hand. On the other side of the gathering, dozens of people are leaning on the bonnets or even lying on the roofs of their vehicles, binoculars to their eyes, gazing down the long U-shaped valley to the east, apparently staring at nothing, until I see with my naked eye another one of those white dots, then a second and a third, moving at great velocity towards us. Several of the observers put down their field-glasses and go to stand behind a cordon of tape, then begin wailing and ululating or banging meal-tubs or metal dishes with sticks and other utensils. The white dots disappear for several seconds, then emerge from a thick patch of green bracken, unmistakably dogs now, beagle-shaped hounds, tearing up the slope towards us. The finishing line is a length of rope draped along the ground, and the first dog hurdles it before bouncing up into its owner's arms, followed by two more dogs, huffing and puffing but seemingly still full of running, followed by a fourth and a fifth, trotting rather than sprinting, then another dog, weary and spent, who walks across the line and sits down, but all are lavished with praise and rewarded with snacks and bowls of water. I put my hands together to applaud the winner, and one of the runners-up lollops over and promptly guzzles my slice of carrot cake then sticks its long, pink, frothing tongue in my cup of tea.

'Sorry, he loves tea. I'll buy you another.'

'Don't worry, I think the dog needed it more than me.'

The owner of the tea-slurping canine explains that the dogs are Border hounds and this is a meeting of the Border Hound Trailing Association. But it's a dying art, she says. 'The young 'uns aren't interested. With their pit bulls and their Rottweilers.' Men walk the course in the morning, dragging an aniseed-soaked rag up hill and down dale, then the dogs are released in their categories and classes, some running as far as seven or eight miles. 'A dog can run in four minutes what a man can walk in half an hour,' she says, and a quick bit of mental arithmetic tells me that a Border hound could complete the Pennine Way in less than a day.

'Do they ever get lost?'

'No. They all wander home. Eventually.'

I'm converting this piece of information into a metaphor for my own journey when I notice that one owner is still standing behind the finishing line, scanning the countryside. 'Come on girl, there's a girl,' she shouts down the valley, then shouts again and rattles a bucket, but the landscape stretching out before her remains open and empty. A few minutes go by. Most of the other competitors and their charges have drifted away towards the food tent or the judging arena. Then finally, a white-and-brown dog pulls itself out of the undergrowth about two hundred yards away, walking, limping even, managing to rally, putting in a little sprint for a few yards when it hears its owner's encouraging yells and the promise of a biscuit, but then slowing again, panting and coughing as it passes me and glancing backwards at the distance behind. Then ten yards short of the finishing line it flops down on the grass, puts its head between its paws, and will go no further.

*

There is a not particularly rewarding anecdote relating to the naming of Once Brewed and Twice Brewed, but for the walker on the Pennine Way it is sufficient to understand that Twice Brewed is the pub and Once Brewed, two hundred yards further back, is the youth hostel. I'd kill for a shower and a kip, and through the glass doors I can see the Tombstone standing upright in reception, waiting by the counter. But the youth hostel doesn't open until four thirty, so I mooch about in the visitors' centre, consoling myself with a vended hot chocolate and pretending to admire the model legionnaires in the glass case.

There isn't a reading today; it's the World Cup final so I've given myself the night off, and as a concession to football fans the landlord of the Twice Brewed has placed a portable telly in the windowsill of the lounge bar. I wander in there for kick-off and sit down next to a Dutch family, who seem to understand that it is their country's duty to play the part of beaten finalists in this competition and accept the narrow defeat as if it were part of an ongoing national tradition. I'm obviously expending energy faster than I can accumulate it; all day I eat vast quantities of carbohydrates, fat and sugar, but I know from my belt that I'm losing weight. I order a Henry VIII-size platter of meat and more meat and a bucket of chips, followed by a whole sponge cake sitting in a bath of custard. I also think that watching a World Cup final in a pub without alcohol is not only contrary but bordering on the perverted, so I break my vow of temperance, and it is under the effect of several pints of local bitter that I meander back along the B6318, also known as the Military Road, aiming to slip into barracks before curfew.

Once Brewed to Greenhead

7 MILES

OS Explorer OL43 West Sheet

Monday 12 July

The police cell I wake in is stuffy and dark. In the blackness I can just about make out the outline of a sink on the wall and a single chair. A guard rattles his keys in the corridor and a door bangs. In the cell next to me somebody coughs. Then silence. I need to pee, but there's no bucket in the corner and there's a bulge in the mattress on the top bunk over my head, and I don't want to disturb whoever's up there and have them come down and smother me with a

pillow, or something worse. I must have done a terrible thing, but what? Is that a window opposite me, or a mirror? My eyes are now making the most of what little light there is, and I notice a hook on the back of the door, which is careless, because I could fashion a noose using the straps on that rucksack or the sleeves of that waterproof jacket. More light enters the room, illuminating a map the size of a rug spread out across the floor, and a compass, and a book full of notes – have I been planning an escape? Several more thoughts of this nature go through my mind until I remember that I am sleeping in the Once Brewed Youth Hostel, that the super-heavyweight convict above my head is the Tombstone, that the crime I committed was to drink too much Twice Brewed ale, and that the sentence for that crime is another fifteen days on the Pennine Way.

I lie awake calculating the miles that have gone by and the miles still to come, and realise for the first time that I'm not looking forward to the morning, because I'm tired, and my back hurts, and there's a pain behind my right knee, and something has been rubbing my shoulder, and my nipples are sore. I go back to sleep thinking that things will be better in the morning, but when morning comes, they aren't. I can't face the communal showers so I splash about in a bit of water in the sink and don't shave, even though I'm absolutely determined not to go home with a beard. In the drying room, the forces of dehydration and the forces of saturation are doing battle by virtue of their smells, and seem to have arrived at a stalemate. Socks on the pipes dangle like petrified exhibits in Mother Shipton's Cave and monstrous leather walking boots stand on the shelves, tongues lolling, laces splayed, like hideous horticultural species in a Victorian glasshouse. Sleeping bags with their inbuilt hoods hang cadaverous and larval from pegs on the walls, surrounded by a tangible aura of dried sweat. A thick woolly jumper slumped across a radiator is beaded with pearls of condensation. Dirty and torn towels of every shape, size and colour are draped from every available hook or rail like flags or pennants rescued from the field of battle after a particularly testing encounter. Back in my cell I go through what has already become a ritual, coating my feet with some kind of podiatric lip-balm to guard against blisters, pulling on the thin surgical-like under-socks then the chunky knitted over-socks, sniffing the armpits of my one, very expensive merino wool undershirt and deciding that its miraculous wicking properties mean it will do another day, filling the water bottles and water bag, folding the map into the appropriate quadrant, applying sunblock. In the medieval poem *Sir Gawain and the Green Knight*, the hero of the story manages to clothe, equip and armour himself in not more than three verses, and he's setting off on an epic journey across the unmapped regions of Dark Ages Britain to do battle with a foe of supernatural colour and superhuman strength. It takes me the best part of an hour to slap on the emollients, tighten straps and replenish supplies, and I'm only walking to Greenhead, less than seven miles to the west.

I perk up a little bit in the dining area where I am diligent in my breakfast routine, adhering to the clearly stated regulations at every stage. It's a long time since I scraped leftovers into a slop-bin or wiped a tabletop with a soapy dishcloth in a public eating space, and there are further duties to be done before leaving, including tidying my room and delivering the bundle of dirty linen to a laundry basket outside reception. When push comes to shove, I find myself thinking, I can still muck in with the rest and haven't become a complete lotus-eating aesthete. And even though I'm unfamiliar with this kind of communal accommodation I've worked out that as far as youth hostels go, Once Brewed, with its TV lounge, games room, laundry, garden, liquor licence and library, is practically the Savoy. I've also realised that the real source of my grumpiness is the fact that I've stupidly volunteered to read this morning at ten o'clock, possibly as some kind of self-imposed punishment for bunking off last night.

In full walking gear and with a big, red, wind-beaten face, photographic evidence records that I do indeed recite poetry to the twenty-three people in the seated area of Once Brewed's open-plan visitors' centre. This ill-advised venture takes place against a soundtrack of hot-drink dispensers, an entire battery of them all approaching percolation climax in unison, plus a looped video presentation of the Romans in Britain on a telly in the corner. During what I imagine to be a lull in the general hubbub, I embark on a sensitive piece about snow angels, only for a coachload of garrulous American school kids to storm the building and form an argumentative scrum outside the toilet door. I can't call it rudeness on their part, because in fairness to them they don't appear to know that I exist, or if they do, probably think I'm some kind of working automaton, Simon the Poet, all part of Northumberland National Park's attempt to present information in a creative and interactive manner. In fact at this moment I wish I *was* a machine, able to go through my routine without feelings or ambition. A woman says to me, 'I'm just going outside to get my two-year-old from the car, but she'll probably cry if she doesn't like it.' I plough on, barely audible above the gift-wrapping of model forts, the ringing of the cash register and the general white noise of tourism. Although I'm reading, I can't help listening to one man's repeated request for very detailed directions to Hexham, then the Information Officer's reply, including her meticulous description of every exit on a particularly complicated roundabout and a list of several other notorious route-finding trouble-spots. Even the sheep in the field to the side are bleating and braying at the top of their vocal range. I read something LOUD and a bit ANGRY to finish with, then as is the way with these things, the moment the reading ends the saboteurs and objectors disperse, even the woolly ones outside, and silence descends. There is £57.50 in the sock, most of it, I suspect, donated in pity.

*

As he criss-crossed the countryside on his trusty horse Gringolet, as well as his sword, his innocence and the blessings of the Round Table, Sir Gawain, the flawed hero of the aforementioned poem, carried with him a shield, the inside of which was painted with the image of the Virgin Mary, as a badge of his faith and a friendly face to look upon in troubled times. I have no such shield and no such devotion, but I do have something in my breast pocket to spur me on across the hard miles. Robert Kirby, my uncle Bob, was a muleteer in the First World War, and he survived, albeit with his lungs full of mustard gas. He couldn't read or write until his wife taught him when he returned home, and he was a fine golfer in his day, but by the time I got to know him he was reduced to sitting in an armchair in the front room, coughing and wheezing and despatching gobbets of thick phlegm into the glowing heat of the coal fire. When I was born I inherited his first name as my middle name. When I was ten I inherited his trusty .177 calibre air-rifle which he kept under the bed to shoot Hitler if he ever had the temerity to enter the village of Marsden and the guts to climb the creaking wooden stairs of a mid-terrace house on Mount Road. And a year or so ago I inherited his war medals. They don't speak of any kind of special gallantry or heroism beyond the call of duty: one bears a laurel and two crossed swords beneath a crown, the other is a coin hanging on a rainbow-coloured ribbon, with George V on one side and a nude horseman on the other cantering over a skull and crossbones, with 'R E KIRBY OF THE WEST RIDING REGIMENT' stamped around the edge. But they are tokens of hardship and risk far greater than anything I can imagine, and I carry them with me as an example of what one blood relative endured just so following generations could go strolling about in the great outdoors without a care in the world. Compared with mushing a packhorse through the trenches of northern France among the flying bullets and exploding bombs, the Pennine Way is a doddle, and quitting for any reason other than actual death would not only be a pathetic failure, it would be a betrayal. That, at least, is my theory.

Military decoration also feels particularly appropriate for today's walk, and in my opinion, even the lowliest foot soldier in the Roman army was surely deserving of some kind of honour or award, one minute strolling the banks of the Tiber or gallivanting in the forum, the next minute patrolling the ramparts of a high wall strung across northern Britain in a howling gale, wearing sandals and a short skirt. (In keeping with the tradition, Newcastle United's Italian signings have suffered a comparable level of foul weather over the years, and for a similar lack of medals.) Publius Aelius Hadrianus arrived in Britain to quell a sustained period of rebellion and incursion, and in AD 122 initiated the building of a great wall to separate the 'barbarians' from his countrymen. There were similar physical boundaries at other edges of the Roman Empire, but lack of timber in these exposed reaches meant construction had to be in stone, a colossal engineering project which would take the best part of a decade, by which time Hadrian had left them to it and gone home to rebuild the Pantheon. Like their roads, there is something direct, no-nonsense and literal-minded about the Wall, in both its conception and assembly. Problem: eighty miles of border trouble. Answer: eighty-mile wall. Problem: big, strong enemy. Answer: big, strong wall. As a declaration of territoriality and power, it takes some beating, but like all such barriers and attempted delineations, be it the Iron Curtain, Offa's Dyke, the Berlin Wall, or the US–Mexico border, it is in the end a shrine to failure. Holding back or penning in human populations is like trying to fence off the weather, and as much a statement of insecurity as one of power. As determined as it is to divide and exclude, a wall is there to be climbed over or knocked down, and the bigger the wall, the greater the challenge. Fifty men were stationed in each milecastle, several hundred cavalry or foot soldiers in each fort, and up to ten thousand along the length of the Wall in total, and for as long as these numbers held firm the structure and the system functioned as planned. But as soon as the Romans left, turning the lights out behind them, people swarmed over and across it in every direction, and even though subsequent regimes have utilised its position and its many strategic advantages, Hadrian's Wall, for all its formidable dimensions, was destined to become nothing more than a line in the sand, a monument to a grand but doomed vision worthy of Ozymandias. Sections which have remained intact, and there are several along today's route, are truly impressive and imposing, especially where the wall seems to be a sympathetic, almost geological extension of the dolerite protrusions themselves, as if the whole thing were a natural phenomenon. In other places the Wall all but disappears; prior to the age of conservation, when need took precedent over pride, it was seen by some as little more than a builder's yard where high-quality material could be obtained for no charge, and the stone was carted away for roads and edifices of all kinds, even for other walls. Thirlwall Castle is one such construction, built from 'recycled' stone, but even that now stands as a ruin and has done for several hundred years, home only to a handful of noisy rooks and a few ghosts.

Des has walked with me. He works for the RSPB, does merchandising for the Wedding Present and is partner of Clare Wadd of cult independent record company Sarah Records fame. There are wheatears everywhere, and a peregrine above Walltown Crags. Like two old, broken records we agree that all music except the music we like is rubbish, and that today's generation of rock stars wouldn't recognise a protest song if it stood up in their soup, etc., etc.

'Is there a lot of call for Wedding Present merchandise these days?'

'Yes, plenty, but it's an ageing fan-base. We don't sell many small or medium T-shirts any more.'

After Thirlwall Castle we head into Greenhead, and through the doors of the Greenhead Hotel. Every village needs a pub and every pub needs a Dave. Dave shakes hands with one hand while pulling a pint with the other. Then he takes me through the back to the 'function room' where I'll be reading tonight, a big pink-and-white space with a low stage, a raised seating area at the back, and a door that closes.

'Great,' I say.

'And I'll get rid of that lot,' he says, pointing to a teetering stack of cardboard trays full of mushrooms and potatoes. Then we share a Masonic-like nod and a wink, acknowledging our unspoken understanding that catering quantities of fresh groceries are not a useful complement to a poetry reading, either as ornament or perfume.

I hadn't met Des before today. He'd just 'taken a punt' and shown up. After a few drinks he disappears and is replaced by Danny (another 'randomer', to use my daughter's term for every person in the world outside her small solar system of family and friends), who comes lugging the Tombstone across the car park and stumbling into the bar. We do a bit of speed-bonding via the subjects of festivals, sport, manual work and vehicles, then I potter over the road to say hello to Wendy, who has set up the reading tonight and offered refreshment to the weary traveller. Wendy lives behind a big wooden door, beyond which is a big old house, full of inglenooks, hearths and laundry creels. On the wall at the foot of the stairs is a blown-up map of the north of England, which she stuck there as a way of reorienting her children, who were brought up in Africa. I like the idea of maps as wallpaper, so much more engaging than repeated patterns of fleurs-de-lys or candy-stripes, although I'm so used to navigating with an upside-down version of this one that I have to do a spot of reorienting myself.

Wendy leads me to what feels like a secret garden, arrived at through ancient doors, along overgrown paths and down rocky steps. She is rearing several ducklings by hand, and they waddle and flap around her ankles as she disappears into a mass of thorny branches then emerges with scratched forearms and a bowl full of gooseberries. She points out various other berries, currants and fruits and tells me to help myself, then wades into another thicket with a basket on her arm. At the bottom of the garden, next to a water-meadow, I rock to and fro on a wicker chair suspended from a sycamore, scooping cherries from a plate as I swish past, balancing a cup of tea in my lap, feeling that a person could be many times poorer than a poet on the Pennine Way, remembering the prayer, 'Lord, may these be the worst of my days.'

*

At the reading I'm thinking about walls and stones and journeys, and read a piece called 'Causeway'. One wing of my family are Cornish, my cousin having married a quarryman from Helston. So we're in Cornwall a lot, and no visit seems complete without a drive to Marazion, then the inevitable traverse to St Michael's Mount, the

island-castle reached via a stone causeway which disappears under the sea then re-emerges at low tide. Visitors can walk over to the island and get marooned there, and it's all very exciting, in an English sort of way. Not long after we'd had our daughter we were out on the island as the tide started to recede, and saw the causeway becoming visible under the water, a very beautifully constructed roadway made from cobbles in the shape of loaves, and it appeared that the water was shallow enough to make the crossing. Which it wasn't, but in the spirit of adventure we decided to be the first ones back across, and because we had an audience we couldn't turn round, so just ploughed on into the ocean, getting lower and wetter and feeling the strong current push against our ankles, then our knees, then our thighs, by which time our daughter was on my shoulders with her legs and arms in a tight knot around my neck. We finally made it to the mainland and were trying to shake ourselves dry, but when we turned around it was as if we had triggered some kind of biblical catastrophe, because suddenly lots of other people were walking into the water, despite our very bad example. Poems don't have to have morals, or even meanings, but the moral of 'Causeway' seems to be something like 'Don't follow me, I don't know where I'm going.' Or, as I saw on someone's T-shirt at a festival a few years ago, 'Don't follow me, you'll end up back at our house.'

Forty-eight people attend the reading, depositing a generous £120.66 in the sock. I eat on my own in the back room, like the pub 'turn' insisting on his contractual meal, gammon and eggs kept warm under a plate long after the kitchen has closed and the fruit machine has been unplugged and beer towels have been draped over the pumps.

Greenhead to Knarsdale

11 MILES

OS Explorer OL43 West Sheet

Tuesday 13 July

I don't want to get up again, but this time it is because I am in a HOTEL. It might not be the Burj Al Arab, but it has a double bed, a double duvet, small cartons of fresh milk next to the mini-kettle, a teacup, and a saucer overlaid with a decorative paper doily. I have eaten every one of the individually packaged stem-ginger cookies and used all the products in the bathroom (including the conditioner) while taking my second shower of the morning before getting back into bed for another half an hour of luxuriating in comfortable idleness. I nod off, and wake up when a train goes rocketing past the window, dragging the curtains with it and all of the air from the room, so for a few seconds I exist in a vacuum.

Under the beams and horse brasses Danny is eating a full English in the bar, with a ketchup bottle standing on a beer mat next to his plate. He has no boots, only a pair of fashionable white trainers, and only a thin waterproof jacket, but he's taken a look at the forecast and decided to walk with me to Knarsdale, 'If that's OK?' Danny is one of a growing majority in this world, i.e. people younger than me. A generation younger, in fact, as is apparent by his attitude and lifestyle. He has responsibilities, including a daughter and a 'proper' job – something involving precision measurements and avionics, the kind that requires learning and sobriety. But he also has a *life*, doing as he pleases when it pleases him without guilt or hand-wringing. He travels intercontinentally, dabbles in extreme mountain-biking, indulges himself at gigs and festivals, and if he fancies walking a bit of the Pennine Way with a poet then why the hell not. He admits as we cross the A69 that until last night he'd never been to a poetry reading before, and that his friends and family were mildly concerned when he announced his intended assignation in the hills with a poet he'd met on the internet. But he's decided to stick around, so I guess that I haven't horrified him too much.

We set off at 9.30 a.m. and by 2 p.m. we are drinking our second pint in the Kirkstyle Inn. So if it really is eleven miles from Greenhead to Knarsdale we must have been walking at a military pace, although we did cheat a bit this morning, picking up the trail where it crossed the main road instead of tramping back up to Haltwhistle Golf Club. Does that mean I'm disqualified?

Perhaps we might have taken more time if there had been more to look at, because in all honesty this isn't the most spectacular or engaging leg of the journey. Yes, the meadows and cow-pastures are pleasant enough. And map-reading around the farmyards and walled fields requires a certain level of mental engagement, and there are some curious little cloughs and valleys to descend into and climb out of, and a few pretty bridges to cross along the way, but nothing to write home about, as they say. Blenkinsopp Common followed by Hartleyburn Common are often cited in the guide books as notorious swamps, and as well as getting bogged down it would be easy to wander off course in what is essentially an un-signposted, featureless plain, where the path lies hidden beneath the grass skirts of thick, knobbly tussocks, and other misleading tracks and channels snake away in the wrong direction. It's dry today; we get lost two or three times but there's enough of a view to navigate by farmhouses on the horizon or more distant hills, and on land which is farmed the extensive matrix of fences and walls usually corrals and steers the wayward rambler towards the right gate or stile eventually. Still, it's always reassuring to spot one of the little green-and-yellow acorns nailed to a post and to see what is clearly a National Trail stretching away in front. At Batey Shield, five men are creosoting six new telegraph poles laid out horizontally in the field – we smell the vapours from two or three hundred yards downwind before we see them. One of the workers puts down his big paintbrush and his bucket of treacle-coloured liquid to explain that a new resident in the area is having electricity installed to a renovated farmhouse somewhere up on the ridge, at his own expense.

'How much will that cost him?'

'A pretty penny.'

The men have a dog with them, one of those yappy Jack Russells with unlimited energy and perpetual enthusiasm, and after doing a couple of circuits of our legs and investigating a smear of sheep shit on Danny's otherwise meticulous trainers it returns to its mini gymkhana, making a clear round of the six wooden poles in a respectable time then coming back for another go. The creosote acts like smelling salts for the memory, reminding me of the many ramshackle constructions I put together with my dad, then daubed with coat after coat of that dark, oily preservative. Like the rabbit hutch, and the tree-house, and several lean-to sheds, all wonky and unstable and built with a dangerous combination of eagerness, impatience and whatever materials came to hand. Our most ambitious structure was a greenhouse. When the leaded sash windows in the house were replaced with uPVC double glazing, we carted the old ones to the bottom of the garden and hammered them together with bent and rusty nails of every length and thickness which had accumulated in a biscuit tin over several generations. For a door we used five sawn-off floorboards and the hinges from a fridge that someone had dumped at the side of the cricket field. How the greenhouse withstood the force of gravity I don't know, let alone the forces of meteorology in the upper Pennines, but it stood its ground for several years, a hothouse for tomatoes, something else I can't smell without being transported back to the early seventies. Some nights I'd still be awake in the small hours, looking through the bedroom window, when my dad came home from a concert or show, disappearing into the black of the garden in his dinner jacket and dickie bow with his pipe in one hand and a watering can in the other. Before the greenhouse finally succumbed to the elements it became an impenetrable jungle, crowded with six-foot-high rose-bay willow-herb and man-eating hogweed, and poking out of the gaps in the roof, the desperate tendrils of aged tomato plants fighting for air and light, still clinging to bamboo canes and rooted in sliced-open grow-bags somewhere deep inside. I also remember the thick, high privet hedge that ran the length of our garden, a sort of dividing line between the lawn and the moor, with civilisation on one side and wilderness on the other. Once, as a punishment (I can't remember what the crime was) my dad made me cut it, all twenty or so yards of it, with a pair of ancient shears which I could hardly lift and barely open. A few hours later, with blistered palms, I watched as he inspected the work, ran his eye and his hand along its trimmed length, saying nothing. Then for reasons which he never explained, he lifted me up and put me down on top of the hedge, so I lay there in its crown, suspended by nothing more than twigs and stalks, looking up at the sky.

*

Marker stones splashed with yellow paint guide the traveller across the valley bottom between the Hartley Burn and the A689. This is another boggy morass in wetter years but navigable today via duckboards, causey paving, some intelligent path-finding and a bit of *It's A Knockout*-style balancing across the wobbly tussocks. At the road there's a sewage works to the right which we don't bother to investigate, then a possible short cut up to Lambley Common, which we also ignore, possibly because I'm feeling guilty about cutting the corner this morning. After climbing to about three hundred metres, the path then stiffens and straightens as it follows the Maiden Way, a Roman road, pointing due south, with the South Tynedale valley running parallel to the left and the South Tyne river flowing north through its corridor. We sit down and eat, with the uninhabited, roadless mass of Glendue Fell followed by the treeless 'forests' of Bruthwaite and Geltsdale at our backs. All through our meal an agitated lapwing and a territorial curlew are protecting their interests, the lapwing

flapping and paddling and piping away on its two-note penny flute and the curlew sounding its ghostly distress whistle while making repeated low-altitude reconnaissance flights over our heads. On the far side of the valley a farmer is herding sheep on a quad bike. At home the sheep are grey, having absorbed the grime in the air and the greyness of the clouds, although it's much cleaner up on Marsden Moor than it was fifty years ago, when soot from the Lancashire mill-towns settled in the heather and the grass and to go for a walk on the tops was to come home filthy. But these sheep are pure white – almost as white as Danny's trainers – especially in the midday sun. Harried by the quad bike and now also by a dog, hundreds of them finally funnel through a gap in a wall and spill out into a lower field, like grains though an hourglass. Crossing Glendue Burn by the stone bridge a man goes past, hurrying up the hill carrying a shotgun and a long-handled axe, but doesn't acknowledge us. As we head through Burnstones I find myself admiring the engorged udders on a very large cow, and Danny says, 'I think you need to go home.'

*

The jukebox in the Kirkstyle Inn, by my reckoning, holds about fifty songs for every house in Knarsdale village, if it is indeed a village and not a hamlet, and possibly not even that. As part of my plan to 'clear my head' I've deliberately left my iPod at home, so this is the first time I've heard recorded music for about a week, and as the money tumbles into the slot and the first guitar chords and drum beats enter my ear, it sounds rapturous and extraordinary, an almost hallucinatory, far-reaching sensory experience. It's as if I'm tripping, a sensation compounded by the notion that every song title seems to be a comment on my personal situation, including 'Should I Stay or Should I Go?', 'Road to Nowhere', 'Many Rivers to Cross', and the compellingly apposite 'Walk This Way'. I say to Danny that it's a pity we didn't bump into each other at Glastonbury earlier in the year, and he points out that it would have been unlikely, not just because there were 170,000 other people there but because at that time we didn't know each other. He seems surprised that I know how to rack the balls in the triangle and which end of the cue to chalk, and when I go three–nil up he tells me that losing to a poet at pool isn't something he'll be bragging about with his friends this coming weekend. Then Wendy turns up in her Noddy-size car, slightly raised at the front by the weight of the Tombstone in the back, and evacuates Danny back to Greenhead, at which point the landlord calls time and I find myself outside on the kerb with a big turquoise suitcase, hoping the weather doesn't change. Suddenly a car pulls up and a man jumps out with a cauliflower in one hand and a lilac-coloured flower in the other.

'Blue sow thistle!' he says to me, holding the flower in my face, then disappearing around the back of the pub. A minute or two later he reappears, minus the vegetable.

'Only found in four places in Britain, that,' he says, waving the flower in front of me again and winking.

'Maybe only three, now,' I say to him, but he's already in the van and away down the road.

*

Josephine Dickinson's house is beyond Alston, almost beyond anywhere it seems, an incongruous brick-built bungalow in a landscape of stone farmhouses and barns, boxed in by a phalanx of dark green pine trees to each side, with west-facing windows looking directly at the incoming weather. Josephine is a poet; I met her twenty years ago on a residential writing course and have bumped into her a couple of times since on the 'circuit'. She was charged by her tup in the field the other day, and although she managed to fend it off with a spade, she's wearing her arm in a sling and nursing some hurt feelings. We wander down to the field with a cup of tea, and watch her very excitable sheepdog perform the wall-of-death around the inside of a breeze-block outbuilding. The tup, who I'm happy to see is on the other side of a sturdy-looking fence, ignores us and goes on nibbling grass. The handful of sheep look ready for shearing to me, some with their fleeces hanging off their backs, like cricketers on a hot day wearing their woolly sweaters tied around their waists, but Josephine says that it will be a couple more weeks before the coats are 'floating', a stage where the wool almost stands off the skin on a layer of fine threads, called the 'rise'. It strikes me as an unusual place to live, this farm, this location, but by every measure Josephine is an unusual person, with an unusual story, which she tells me in her living room, surrounded by tottering piles of books and in the presence of three inquisitive cats. Some years ago, she and her boyfriend were living what is sometimes characterised by the media as a 'chaotic lifestyle' when they were given a small flock of geese as a present. The geese were supposed to be kept in a pen for a few days to remind them where home was, but on the warm and bright morning after they arrived, Josephine decided to let them out for a bit of fresh air, and away they sailed, over the wall and off down the valley. Unable to round them up on her own she screwed her courage to a point and went to the brick-built bungalow between the dark stands of pine trees, to ask the notoriously ill-tempered farmer Douglas for a helping hand, and he astonished her by coming to her rescue and assisting in the recapture attempt. The day after, she approached the bungalow again, on tiptoe this time, hoping to push a thank-you note through the letter box then skedaddle. But the door opened and Douglas invited her in, and within a week she was living with him, and not long after, they were married. It was a coming together of needs and wants, Douglas cooking and caring for Josephine and supplying his highly accurate veterinary syringe so Josephine could measure out reduced dosages of medication until she was clean, and Josephine's luminosity – something noticed by everyone who meets her – brightening the dark corners and shadows of Douglas's life. More remarkable is the fact that when Josephine walked into his house and closed the door behind her, she was forty-one and Douglas was eighty-six. She pulls out an album, and shows me wedding photographs of the happy couple, which in any other family would be images of the smiling bride and her proud father, or doting grandfather even, except their knowing faces and their intertwined hands and the language of their bodies tell a different tale. There's a moving symmetry to the story: when Douglas died he was ninety-two, Josephine having nursed him through his last days, and Douglas having reawakened her poetic instincts – she's published four books since that first meeting. She closes the album and slides it back into the bookshelf. I say that she must miss him, but she doesn't catch the words because her head is turned and she can't see my lips, and when she can't see my mouth she can't understand me, because Josephine is deaf. And to add yet another twist to the story, she is also a classically trained pianist. I ask her if she can play some Chopin, and after searching through a pile of sheet music she sits down in front of the upright Boyd & London, straightens her back, places her fingers on the keys, and plays. Like with the jukebox earlier in the day, it feels like another hyper-sensory experience, but more so this time, the kind of music that God must hear, no matter how busy or distracted, because it comes out of hundreds of square miles of nothingness, out of the emptiness of the hills and the silence of the moors, and from the most unlikely hands.

*

I am driven to the reading through heavy rain at terrifying speed by a local woman who 'knows the roads'. The venue is Yew Tree Chapel B&B in Slaggyford, with its amazing stained-glass windows made by David, the owner. Doves are perched on the garden gate and the trellised archway, as if in welcome. Every time the little bell rings it makes the sound of someone entering a situation-comedy corner shop, then Mary answers the door and shows audience members to their seats, either around the living room or on the stairs or the galleried balcony, even in the pulpit. The reading is prefaced with a musical recital for piano and flute. A clock chimes on the half-hour and the hour. My allocated reading position is a high-legged red swivel-chair in the corner of the room; pushing off with my feet, I make a couple of anti-clockwise revolutions, letting the wooden beams and the wall-lights and the high ceiling orbit around me for a few moments, letting the centrifugal force spin blood to the outer edges of my brain before slowing and coming to a halt in front of the twenty-nine waiting faces. And then I begin.

Knarsdale to Garrigill

10 MILES

OS Explorer OL43 West Sheet, OL31 West

Wednesday 14 July

I wake early in the company of cats, one on the bed, one on top of the wardrobe and another in the Tombstone with its head on the money sock, guarding the £148 takings from last night's reading. I managed to launder about a third of the pound coins with Dave ('Never say no to change') at the Greenhead Hotel, but the amount of cash I'm hauling across the country is becoming a bit of a headache. The increasingly thick wad of notes might not be a huge strain on the rucksack but it's weighing heavily on my mind, and I've started daydreaming about caching it in the earth, like foxes do with dead rabbits and voles, to return to during times of need. I could leave it in the Tombstone, I suppose; the Tombstone has no lock, but does contain a repellent quantity of festering underwear and rancid socks, and anyway, I'm living among *the kind people*, people who've voluntarily given their time, their energy, their front rooms, their beds, their cooked breakfasts and their towels in exchange for nothing more than the recital of a dozen or so poems, most of which (as one lady felt obliged to point out to me after last night's reading) don't even rhyme. Perhaps it's embarrassment, then, that's making me carry a sheaf of readies down the spine of the Pennines instead of simply asking someone to stick it in the bank for me or swap it for a cheque, though when I make a quick mental calculation of how much I've spent on coats, boots, socks, gadgets, salves, maps and other assorted necessaries, I'm still a long way down on the deal. Lying awake among the purring cats and the sound of wood pigeons in a tree outside, my mind moves from stocktaking and auditing to a more general consideration of my progress so far. To date, I've walked about eighty miles, just less than a third of the way, in six days, and apart from a few minor aches and pains, I feel fine. On the first day I decided to keep a score of mental and physical well-being, giving myself a grade out of ten at the end of every leg, ten being human perfection, zero being dead. I was expecting wild oscillations of both mood and health, but so far it's been a steady seven or eight on both counts. Can I walk the same distance twice more? Yes, I reckon I can. Will I finish the Pennine Way? Well, say it softly, but I think I just might. And on that smug note I roll over and indulge in another hour's kip.

*

A further reason for the sense of quiet confidence is that today's stretch is a bit of a dolly, a saunter of ten miles in an unwavering direction along the banks of the South Tyne, a gentle climb of no more than a hundred metres all told with a disused railway line to guide the way, and A TOWN, Alston, about halfway along, with cake shops and pubs. Only a week ago a ten-mile walk would have been an expedition, but now it's a rest, even a reward, and the only foreseeable hindrance to progress today will be indolence.

David, a friend, has come to walk with me. He's been staying somewhere in the eaves of Yew Tree Chapel and descends the stairs with wet hair and the remains of breakfast-in-bed on a tray. The temptation would be to strike directly south from here but having cheated once already, if only by a few hundred yards, I dutifully insist that we go back to Knarsdale before beginning in earnest. There may be wind up on the hills but down here in the valley bottom it is sheltered and still, and even though the ground is wet and the river lively from last night's downpours, the sun comes out and the elevated path manages to steer a course between waterlogged ditches and flooded fields. In fact dead rabbits are the only obstacle for the first hour, at least one every couple of hundred yards, all speckled brown fur and little white arses, fully stretched, back legs and front legs pointing in opposite directions with no obvious signs of disease or attack. I turn one over with the toe end of my boot expecting to see some bloody wound to the throat or a pair of bulging 'myxie' eyeballs, but its eyes are closed, its face at rest and its pelt perfectly intact. Hundreds more are hopping around in the grass on the hillside so I guess dead ones are a mathematical inevitability, but why so many of them should be lying prostrate along the Pennine Way remains a mystery.

The old green-and-cream wooden station-house on the west side of the line at Slaggyford is crying out to become a cafe, but unfortunately for us no one has yet seized the entrepreneurial initiative. Somewhere above the old Roman fort at Whitley Castle we are suddenly enveloped by a flood of sheep streaming through an open gate, followed by a young farmer on his quad bike who looks like early Bob Dylan. I think at first he's come to bollock us for trespassing, but he's just passing the time of day. In exchange for a home-made shortbread biscuit he lets me perch on the bike for a photograph, and if I'd had a Victoria sponge to offer would have probably let me take it for a spin around the field as well. A couple of times he mentions a place called Cross Fell and points with a farmer's finger in a southerly direction, but I'm too interested in the gearing mechanism of his all-terrain hill-buggy to ask questions or listen to advice, and after a few more biscuits he revs up and goes roaring off after his flock.

The route here isn't exactly a tax on the body or a test of the mind, but I'm not complaining, the memory of going astray in the Cheviots still being very clear and not an experience I'm in a hurry to repeat. In fact a walker would have to be wearing a blindfold to get lost today, since several other routes and features running parallel to the Way act as handrails or stabilisers, including the South Tyne River, the A689, the South Tynedale Railway, the South Tyne Trail, and Isaac's Tea Trail, a walk 'in the footsteps of legendary itinerant tea-seller Isaac Holden', a former lead miner forced to seek alternative employment when the industry collapsed. Some reports of Holden's life also suggest that he sold poems to passengers on the railway as a way of raising money, and for a few miles I muse on the idea that I too have made a similar transition from lead to poetry and tea. The area around Alston was once a hub for the lead-mining industry, the earth being rich in deposits, and the landscape is scarred with evidence of extraction, some of it going right back to the Romans and even beyond. In the 1800s when the mining was at its peak, as well as being used for bullets, pewter and poisons, much of the malleable and waterproof element was being applied to the roofs and windows of large buildings such as churches and schools, and for a brief period during the summer of 1976 me and a bunch of friends were stripping it back off again. In one of the first poems I ever wrote, 'Without Photographs', I remember how we unearthed the makings of a small, illicit foundry buried beneath an old door under Bank Bottom mill in the village. It took us a while to work out what the brazier, bricks, pans and ladles had been used for, until we unrolled a length of sacking and two shiny blocks of lead spilled out at our feet. Then the penny dropped. So for most of that hot, unending summer we were a regular industry, building fires, melting down coils of lead flashing in a battered old saucepan and turning out stacks of gleaming, silver-coloured ingots that dimmed to a slate grey as they cooled. The moment when the lead suddenly lost all its solidity and ran like mercury across the base of the pan was never less than miraculous, an alchemical transformation, and before the liquid became sluggish and slow we spooned it into the well or 'frog' of a regulation red brick. And I learned the hard way that if any water was trapped in the well, the hot lead spat back in a volley of fiery pellets at the moment of contact. When one of those pellets hit me on the side of the knee it seared a hole in my skin; I still have the burn and have watched it migrate a couple of inches south over the intervening years. When the ingots were finally tipped or tapped out, they were indented or embossed with the names of famous brickworks, names like Accrington and Stewartby, and one highly prized brick (highly prized by me, anyway) carried the word ARMITAGE. The thrill was all in the process rather than the product, though we did eventually develop the commercial interests of the company, taking the blocks to a no-questions-asked scrap-metal merchant down the valley and weighing them in for cash. The lead, living up to one of its most famous characteristics, was not light, and we must have looked a suspicious and even comical bunch, four of us on the service bus in our shorts, in charge of a holdall we could hardly lift, even with two people to each handle. On one occasion I snatched up a carrier bag and jumped on the bus but the four lead ingots it contained remained on the pavement, resolute and inert. It was stealing, I admit, though the metal was usually taken from dilapidated woolsheds or the Electric Cinema which had collapsed after a snowstorm. But the guilt was always offset by the feeling that we were doing something 'constructive' with our time, as instructed, and anyway, the lead was so soft and compliant, and offered itself readily to our hands. It was also my first experience of manual labour, and of the manufacturing industry, and of the work ethic, going home filthy every night but glowing inside with the satisfaction of a mission accomplished and a job well done.

And now I write poems and drink tea.

*

Unfortunately we don't have any tea with us when we stop for lunch by the war memorial just east of the river in Alston, only water bottles or my 'drip', and anyway it wouldn't feel right to be sipping Earl Grey or a herbal infusion in front of the names of those who gave their lives to the cause. We've just clambered along ten yards of broken-down wall which the land-owner is obviously in no hurry to repair, and for reasons that I can't explain I've

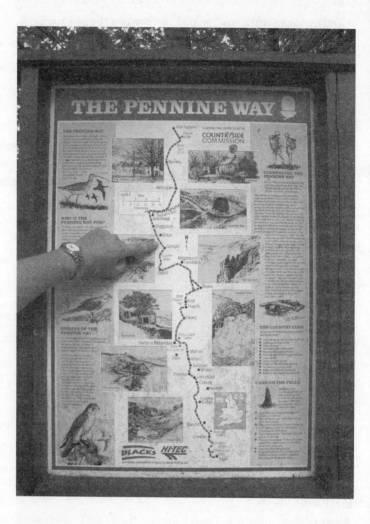

taken several photographs of a goat. There's another photo opportunity on the other side of the bridge, the same sign as the one in Kirk Yetholm, showing the Pennine Way as a dotted line winding among drawings of natural features and local wildlife, and this time I'm able to point to a position at least a third of the way down the trail, between the curlew and the merlin. For the next four or five miles the path follows the river, sometimes running close to the water, sometimes staying a couple of contours above it, and the river itself is the view, shallow and gossipy where it skitters across pebbles and stones, then soupy and slow in a dam or basin, then parting around some island of boulders colonised by reeds and ferns, then taking a wide arc around a sandbank or shingle beach, then snaking among the exposed roots of trees before tumbling over a ledge in the bedrock, diving into a pool of dark water before resurfacing as bubbles and froth a little further downstream. Almost everything is in bloom and in leaf, thick with life. I'm not a birdwatcher in the sense of keeping a list but I like to know what I see when I see it, and along here that includes dipper, lapwing, grey wagtail, the momentary iridescent flash of a kingfisher – just a travelling, coloured blur rather than the definable outline of an actual bird – then an enormous heron, packing up its one-man tent in a huff of flapping feathers, rowing away over the tree-tops, and when I look back a minute or so later, coming back to pitch camp on the same reef of mud. Josephine has joined us at Bleagate, telling stories of suicides, adultery and apparitions as we pass various tumbledown farms, and just before the path crosses the bridge back to the west bank of the river we meet Mike and his golden retriever waiting to guide us the last couple of miles.

The approach to Garrigill clearly hasn't been orchestrated by the tourist board, because after the textbook tranquillity of the waterside the path sneaks furtively through what looks like a tipping area with heaps of spoil and rusting machinery to both sides, but it's only a temporary diversion before the settlement appears up ahead, with its low stone houses and village green. For the first time in the journey I'm pimping myself in return for clothing, and have remembered to wear my 'Count Me Inn – Save the George and Dragon' T-shirt. Despite the fact that the rain has started to fall I unzip my coat to demonstrate my solidarity with the cause, until Mike points out that unfortunately it's too late and that time has been called at Garrigill's only licensed premises once and for all. The downpour also means that the reading won't take place on the green, as was hoped, but in the village hall. They'd erected a marquee for the event, hoping for one of those summer evenings from the rose-tinted past, but already water is cascading from the awning, the wind has got hold of a couple of guy ropes, and a sizeable puddle has developed in front of the entrance. I feel like a bad Jesus, arriving too late, bringing a black cloud.

Mike is married to Janette, who was once my boss, in a previous century. The last time she saw me I was a trainee probation officer on loan to Huddersfield Social Services for a stint with their Fostering and Adoption team, but all that feels so long ago now it could have been another life. So it's peculiar when she recognises me, because as far as those days go I barely recognise myself. Not only do Mike and Janette have a dedicated guest room with a big bed and a soft mattress, they also have an en-suite wet room and a do-whatever-you-want-for-a-couple-of-hours policy, so I stay under the scalding jet of the shower until the hot water runs out then lie down with the intention of getting a couple of hours' sleep before the reading. When sleep doesn't happen I pull out my notebook and begin making a record of the day's happenings, and remember that on two or three occasions people have mentioned tomorrow's walk, over somewhere called Cross Fell. Bob Dylan mentioned it while I was ogling his quad bike, and so did a man leaning over his garden fence the other side of Alston, smirking as he pronounced its name, and Josephine was polite but enigmatic on the subject as we glanced at the anvil-shaped profile on the horizon, and now I come to think about it, every time I've looked in that direction, all I've seen is a solid dark barrier to the south, barring the way ahead. I thought I'd figured out all the trouble-spots on this walk before setting off, places like the Cheviots and Tan Hill and Kinder Scout, factored them into my itinerary and made adequate mental preparations for each encounter. But somehow Cross Fell hadn't been on my radar at all, which is a pretty glaring omission I now realise, pulling out one of the guide books and discovering that it is in fact the highest point in the Pennines and also the highest summit in England outside the Lake District. Not only that, it was once known as Fiend's Fell, some believing it to be the haunt of devils and demons, and is prone to impenetrable mists caused by a recurring cloud formation known as the Helm Bar, and to a shrieking or wailing in the air, brought about by a local wind. Today's saunter along that pleasant river valley was obviously one of those little games the Pennine Way likes to play, lulling walkers into false states of confidence, softening them up just prior to the next intimidating ordeal. When I peer out, I can't quite see the Fell from the back window, but the darkness outside seems to be emanating from its direction, like a shadow, and when I unfold the map and spread it out on the hand-stitched bedspread, the contrast couldn't be greater, the quilt being a thing of great colour and beauty and precision and love, the map being a big square of nothingness except contours and white space and spidery blue streams like varicose veins. It's like one of those maps of the sea, all very meaningful, presumably, at some level, but to the layman in a boat, essentially just a vast area of cold featureless water without land or hope. I feel my heart sinking to my heels, and my nerves tightening slightly, and what there was of my smile dissolving from my lips.

*

Walking down the side of the river in the early evening (the river loud and excited with the water from Cross Gill, Cross Gill being an outlet from what I now imagine to be the rain-factory of Cross Fell), Janette asks a man fiddling around under a car if he is coming to the reading. Only his legs are visible, a pair of scuffed boots at the end of a pair of oily blue jeans, and from somewhere beneath the engine, through the open bonnet, a voice replies, 'Er, no, not this time,' as if this kind of thing happened every night and he'll be sure to catch Les Murray or Wendy Cope on Tuesday. The George and Dragon is indeed well and truly closed, although some Banksy-esque wag has painted a very convincing open door on the boarded-up entrance, and scenes of boozy conviviality

on the boards at each window. I also think the same *trompe-l'œil* effect has been applied to the Post Office, with its battered wooden door and barricaded window complete with a slot for the postbox, until Janette points out that it's real. With its pebbledash surround and stencilled sign, the business is either very old, or has been attacked on many occasions, or represents a kind of knowingly antiqued regional chic, or possibly a combination of all three. In the village hall they've wheeled in a bar on castors with beer pumps G-clamped to the counter connected to barrels of local ale. Four squaddies are drinking at one table but they clear off at the mention of the word poetry. Someone tells me they are sleeping in the roof space but doesn't explain why. The hall fills up over the next hour, until sixty-two people are sitting on an assortment of chairs and tables of

varying size and style. It's about one third of the entire population of Garrigill, apparently, the only notable absentee being the village poet, who I can only assume has decided to stay at home and sulk. £98.45 finds its way into the sock and Mike won't let me pay for my beer. Several people leaning on the piano tell me that they'll accompany me up Cross Fell tomorrow, but they've all been drinking. It's late when we spill outside to make our way back to the house, on a night without moonlight in a village without street lights at a time when most people have gone to bed. Waiting for Mike to lock up I see a swinging torchlight moving away down the street. It's Josephine, heading off through the village, to walk the three or four miles back to her house down the black valley, alongside the dark river, alone and in her silence.

Garrigill to Dufton

16 MILES

OS Explorer OL31 West Sheet, OL19 North

Thursday 15 July

It's the end of the night and I'm being driven by a friend, Malone, back along country roads to the remote East Cumbrian village of Maulds Meaburn. It's a few miles from the official Pennine Way but Malone is an acquaintance of 2004's AA B&B Landlady of the Year, the well-named Mrs Kindleysides, owner of Meaburn Hill Farmhouse, whose evening meals and cooked breakfasts are not to be sniffed at. Dufton, the end-point of today's walk, is disappearing in the rear-view mirror. A former mining centre, it seems more charming and softer-edged than other places with a similar history. Made a conservation area in 2005, it is, in outward appearances at least, a picture-perfect community, with its annual show, village green, lawned verges and local pub, the Stag Inn, where I've sunk a couple of pints of Black Sheep in front of an open fire. It also boasts a village hall to be proud of, a tidy black-and-white-painted, stone-built, slate-roofed construction at the heart of the settlement, ideal for a midweek poetry reading and comfortably housing the sixty-one-strong audience, who paid a total of £153.35 for the pleasure. For their money they heard me recite a number of 'journey poems' including a piece called 'Before You Cut Loose', based on a story my mother told me after returning from a hiking holiday in Ireland. Walking out of a village one day, a dog started to follow them, a black Labrador, and stayed with them for several miles despite well-intentioned discouragement, including verbal abuse, threats of physical violence with a big stick and stones hurled in its direction. After twenty miles the dog was still with them, and out of a sense of both guilt and Christian obligation (they were members of a church rambling society) they resigned themselves to getting to their destination, finding a taxi and taking the dog back. But as they began their descent from the hills and walked into a distant town, the dog suddenly sprinted off in front of them and pushed open the door of a house, where it lived. The story has always had a parable-like quality to me, the dog's loyalty and resolve winning out over so many misguided interventions, its stamina and its sense of direction seeing it home in the end, and given the events of my day, I read it with a sense of irony rather than satisfaction, events involving lots of mist, lots of rain, a lost poet with none of the dog's qualities whatsoever and four scantily clad strangers on a Pennine summit. From Malone's car I glance up towards Cross Fell, high above Dufton, its angular forehead now basking in the pink sunset, its characteristic shape now visible for the first time in twelve hours, the outline of its sloped shoulders and jutting brow now clear and defined under a cloudless evening sky, and under my breath I say, 'You bastard.'

*

Cross Fell is a truly terrible place. The word 'fell' conjures up images of Wordsworthian hills, their noble peaks and timeless profiles reflected in clear tarns and placid lakes, their foothills adorned with hosts of golden daffodils in full bloom. Cross Fell is some abhorrent strain of that particular fell species, the Caliban version, illegitimate and monstrous and exiled to the other side of the M6. Of course I haven't yet formed this opinion when I rise at about seven in the morning and blast myself awake under the hot power-shower. The spare bedroom is on the ground floor at the front of the house, and while I'm going through the now mechanical process of applying various lotions and creams and practising expert origami with the map, I can hear a bit of a commotion outside. When I pull back the curtains, six or seven people are standing on the pavement or sitting on the wall, people I vaguely recognise from last night's reading, whose pledges of company and support were more than just the beer talking, it seems. Giving them a nod and a wave I can't decide if I'm the Pied Piper, about to lead a gaggle of locals out of town, or Edward Woodward in *The Wicker Man*, about to be guided by locals to a terrible fate up on the hill. It also puts me in mind of the scene in Monty Python's *Life of Brian* when his mum goes outside and says to the waiting disciples, 'He's not the Messiah, he's a very naughty boy.'

Much as I appreciate their backing, not everyone in the party looks particularly well equipped for an assault on a mountain which rises to just under three thousand feet above sea level. One woman tells me she is in training for a trek to Machu Picchu, the pre-Columbian Inca ruins which stand at an oxygen-starved altitude three times higher than Cross Fell, but she is wearing jeans and a cardigan and turns back just short of the one-mile mark. A breathless man with a very red face also turns tail not long afterwards, signalling his resignation with a hand gesture, his mouth and throat being fully employed with the business of breathing, and others fall away at each passing stile or cattle-grid. Admittedly this is a long and arduous ascent. All the guide books describe the old Corpse Road from just under the neb of Cross Fell to Garrigill village as boring at the very least, and at worst gruelling and tortuous, the pebble and cinder track being hard on the feet and the endless, unchanging landscape being hard on the eye. And that's walking downhill! Uphill it is all those things magnified, and I can't blame my escorts for eventually peeling off, especially since they're not actually walking *with* me. Because for the first time on this journey I realise that I've developed something of a regular pace, and not a slow one, a pace and also a rhythm of motion that feels very natural in relation to the weight in the rucksack, the ground underfoot, the angle of incline, the fuel in my belly and several other variables related to the scientific principles of bipedalism. At a certain speed everything feels to be working smoothly, the motor purring, the escapement ticking, the cogs turning, everything at its operational best; to slow down isn't painful but it's certainly annoying, and I find myself sympathising with those lorry drivers on the motorway who get to within a couple of yards of the car in front, flashing their lights and honking their air-horns, drivers who would prefer to plough through the back of a family saloon rather than lose revs and momentum. So by the time I get to Pikeman Hill, having climbed about a thousand feet and covered a good three miles in little more than an hour, I'm out on my own. I kick the ground with my boot and scratch around at the side of the path for fluorspar, the bluish mineral which was once considered a useless by-product of the lead-mining process but is now mined in its own right and is reported to 'litter' this track, but I can't see anything remotely colourful or attractive. Perhaps fluorspar needs sunlight to bring it to life and there certainly isn't any of that around. If anything the sky has dimmed since this morning, and the air has become colder and sharper, partly because of the height, obviously, but also on account of the deteriorating conditions. I feel the occasional drop of rain, and up ahead a bank of cloud not only obscures the head of Cross Fell but appears to be overflowing down its shoulders and upper slopes. The route across it seems pretty straightforward on the map, but that's only because I've highlighted it in dayglo orange. In reality, the path in front of me arcs away into that horrible cloud, and experience tells me that a track like this, as defined and unmistakable as it is right now, will simply peter out at that height. And except for the exaggerated chain of diamonds representing the Pennine Way, the only other cartographical features for the foreseeable future are curricks, cairns, sink-holes, shake-holes, hushes and shafts, the first two being piles of stones like unmarked graves, the other four being things you can fall down and die. I'm trying to process all this information and quantify my chances of actually making it to the other side when I see that I'm not on my own, because after politely walking at a more sociable pace for the first mile or so, Richard has now broken free from the peloton of stragglers and deserters, and put his foot down. Richard is in computers, something he can do without living in the big city, and has brought with him his camera and his dog. He's been over Cross Fell several times, he tells me, and although he doesn't want to walk all the way to Dufton he'll come with me to the summit, or just below it, and point me in the right direction. I greet his arrival and news of his experience of this territory with a kind of studied coolness, but from the moment he hoves into view it is my secret plan not to allow him out of my sight until he has delivered me safely over the hill. It's now only a question of how far I will go to ensure his co-operation, be it the feigning of some sudden injury, a crude cash payment or the promise of a thousand virgins and eternal life on the other side of the mountain.

We kick on up the gradient, the dog fussing here and there, forward and back. A couple of gamekeepers drive by in what appears to be some kind of amphibious landing craft, like a big bathtub on wheels. They're laying down piles of feed for the grouse, mounds of white, flaky-looking stuff like crystallised porridge oats. They're also checking us out, I think, making sure we don't stray from the path, disturbing the birds and disrupting revenue streams. Long Man Hill comes and goes on the left. Looking occasionally towards the lowland we've left behind, the odd shaft of sunshine, like a searchlight, tracks across a meadow or makes a sweep of a valley, and there's certainly a brighter, drier, calmer world to the north. But we're heading south, up the mountain, into the cloud. The path is silver against the dark green of the moor, and I can see it swing round to the west, rejecting a steep, direct approach to the top and circling instead around the collar of the hill, below a scree slope and a line of tumbled boulders, looking for the best angle of attack. The ground to either side of the track is gouged and scarred where shovels and picks have gone in search of valuable metals and where machines have clawed and buried their way into the earth. Spoil is heaped in useless, ugly piles, half-hearted causeways lead nowhere, disused quarries have filled with rain, low tumbledown walls mark the sites of abandoned buildings or collapsed sheds. It's ghostly and depressed. Nothing has properly healed, and some of the stones and workings have oxidised to a rusty red, the colour of dried blood.

Greg's Hut, perched at the end of the track, is described variously as a bothy, a shelter, a refuge and an ex-mine shop. Whatever its true designation or provenance it is certainly a welcome sight, the grey stonework acting as camouflage against the grey landscape for much of the approach, but on closer inspection being quite a characterful cottage-style building, like a hillside dwelling belonging to some mad and ancient man of the mountains, with an ornate chimney, painted yellow window frames and a lime-green door. There's even the hint of a walled garden with a couple of fir trees within it, the trees being the only vertical features in a landscape dominated by the horizontal, except of course for the two sweating and steaming walkers who push open the hut door and close it behind them. With my voice recorder I make a tour of Greg's Hut like an estate agent valuing a new property. The vestibule is a lean-to lobby-cum-log-shed containing several spades and, well, logs. This opens into a surprisingly light and airy stone-flagged common room or function area, with plastic chairs tipped up against the wall, like a classroom at the end of the school day. There's a solid-looking table which appears to have been constructed from breeze-block and Meccano, and a string of Tibetan prayer flags which, if the blue sock pegged in the middle is anything to go by, also functions as a washing line. Above the mantelpiece there's a portrait of Greg himself, and a plaque, and on the windowsill a bottle of amber-coloured liquid, labelled PEE. There's probably some very sensible, survivalist reason why the stranded walker should pee in a bottle rather than on the several thousand acres of empty moorland outside, but for the moment I can't work out what it is. The third room, furthest from the door, is the business end, with a stove, nightlights, candles, kindling, matches, walking magazines (to either read or burn depending on the severity of the crisis), and a raised wooden platform which I describe as the 'stage'. 'Sleeping platform,' corrects Richard. Obviously my inclination to see every structure on this trip as a potential venue for a poetry reading is getting the better of me. There's also a palm cross resting on two nails above the fire. The visitors' book is full of tales of woe and endurance, of which Greg's Hut is always the saviour. An entry from a few days ago reads, 'PS If you see Simon Armitage, tell him he nicked my idea.' Finding my pen I make the point that the idea of a book based on a long journey was originally Homer's, then we break out the biscuits and the flask.

*

Unless you have been lost in mist on the moors or in the hills, it is probably difficult to understand the true horror of the experience or to fully sympathise with the sufferer. Admittedly, it is not the same level of danger as stumbling around in Death Valley without a water bottle, or dangling from a rope down the north face of the Eiger, or being shot at by bandits in the Khyber Pass, or a million other such situations associated with intrepid adventure or extreme sports. But it is frightening, and on the few occasions it has happened to me, I have noticed a very alarming and rapid change in my psychology, as if the claustrophobia and disorientation brings about a particular *condition*, the symptoms of which include fear, panic and loss of logical thought, but also less expected and harder-to-define sensations akin to sadness and melancholy, something like hopelessness but also close to grief. In other words, it is *upsetting*, and as we leave the foursquare Alamo of Greg's Hut and begin the climb to the top, I feel the sorrow and unhappiness welling up inside me, anticipating what is to come. And it's a matter of minutes before we enter the realm of mist, because the cloud base has a surprisingly well-defined border, so after only ten yards the view behind us is no longer available as a reference point, and the view ahead is nothing but a silvery, swirling mass, and we have disappeared. It is also raining, or at least the air is very wet, and the gusts of wind now sheering across the upper slopes are laden with water vapour, so we are soaked. Right on cue the track, which had narrowed to a path, then to vague ruts in the ground, gives up the ghost. We make more strides, onto what feels like a plateau, and now there are six or seven trails to choose from, none of them especially convincing. Something about the acoustics, or perhaps the air pressure, tells me that we are *on* but not yet *at* the summit, and from the guide books I digested this morning and a quick squint at the map I know there are another hundred yards or so to walk before reaching the stone shelter at the top. Richard takes the lead, which is his prerogative, having been up here many times, but instinctively I disagree with the direction. After five minutes I say, 'I don't think this is right.' I don't think Richard thinks it's right either, but we don't have a better plan, so we walk some more, until even the dog looks a little distrustful, and I say, 'Shouldn't we be walking uphill?' Richard says, 'This is uphill, isn't it?' And I say, 'We're going downhill, I reckon,' though now he's said it, I'm no longer confident of my own judgement. Because when the clouds fold in and the horizon disappears, it's not only the internal compass that goes haywire, it's also the altimeter, the gyroscope, the chronometer, the sextant and the inclinometer. And the lid that battens down the emotions, keeps them locked away and packed tight in a little box, that flies open as well.

The one advantage of being lost today is that for as long as Richard doesn't know where he is, he can't go home. He's offered to get me to the top, from which the subsequent peaks of Little Dun Fell and Great Dun Fell mark an obvious and unmissable route to the south-east, so in my own mind, until those summits and the path which apparently forms a kind of trapeze between them becomes visible, or unless the cloud miraculously lifts and the whole of the north of England becomes an illuminated page rolled out before me, he's going nowhere. We try to retrace our steps, but we've no idea which direction we came from, so we have to guess. We find a place which looks vaguely like a place we saw a quarter of an hour ago, a stone next to a peaty ditch, in a terrain which is all stones and peaty ditches, then make an exaggerated and purposeful turn to the left, as if being assertive and decisive might rescue our situation. I'm now in charge, or at least I'm in front, my instincts having pulled rank on Richard's experience. A truly impressive Dalek-like cairn comes forward out of the cloud,

about eight foot tall. But a cairn is just a pile of stones, not a signpost, not a policeman, not a tourist information centre, and after failing to find it on the map we have to leave what little comfort it offered and let it disappear behind us into the void. Finally there's nothing else for it but to pull out the GPS device and to convince ourselves that it isn't lying. It seems to be pointing in absolutely the wrong direction, to a laughable degree, so much so that it is a triumph of mind over matter to just believe in its assessment of our position let alone follow its course, but five minutes later we find the trig point and the cross-shaped shelter, and hunker down out of the driving wind.

*

On some days, the guide books promise, the summit of Cross Fell offers views as far as the Solway Firth. It probably does not need saying that today is not one of those days. Visibility is at most five yards; seeing my hand in front of my face is about as good as it is going to get today, and even though we've finally made it to the top of the hill, there's no obvious track leading away into the distance, and absolutely no prospect whatsoever of lining up the next two fells. I know for certain that if Richard turns back now I will turn back with him, because I simply don't have the bottle to go wandering into that mist on my own, and if I turn back, all the scheduled readings and offers of hospitality will collapse like dominoes, the whole project will unravel, and I will have failed. I don't know how I convince Richard to walk a little bit further, whether it is through some humiliating confession, or if he hears the quavering desperation in my

voice, or smells the fear, or feels compelled by some ineffable sense of obligation to go the extra mile, but we set off together. And get lost again, this time in a bewildering moonscape of angular boulders and strewn rocks. Unknowingly, I've gouged open an old cut on my finger with my thumbnail and made it bleed. Feeling the brunt of the wind, almost an updraught, I'm guessing we're on some sort of escarpment or ridge, but no matter which direction we walk in we can get no higher or lower, just further into the rocky wilderness, deeper into the milky atmosphere. The melancholy comes over me again, the dismal misery of not knowing where I am, or perhaps losing any sense of *who* I am, as if the mist is bringing about an evaporation of identity, all the certainties of the self leaching away into the cloud. I don't cry, but I could easily let it happen, if I wanted to, and I'm close to wanting to. Out comes the GPS, which this time offers an even more stupefying conclusion to our predicament, but with the compass in one hand, balanced and delicate, and the map in the other, we follow the dithering red needle for twenty yards, fifty yards, two hundred yards, a quarter of a mile, and eventually we are heading downhill. Not only that, we seem to be on a path, and on that path, in the distance, are human beings, four of them, plus a couple of dogs, although it could be a mirage because two of the figures appear to be semi-naked and the other two not particularly dressed for a hike on the moors. The four apparitions are also jogging, jogging towards us, and suddenly remembering a very loose arrangement concerning four fell-runners agreeing to meet me on the way to Dufton, I go running towards them, bounding along the stone slabs. Receiving them like long-lost friends I give one of them a big hug, the nearest one, not even one of the two women but one of the slightly surprised men, and introduce Richard to these four wonderful people whose names I don't know and who might be *my* fell-runners but might just as easily be *random* fell-runners, bemused by the rapturous welcome and the uncontrollable display of back-slapping and hand-shaking and cheek-kissing coming from my direction. And suddenly there are even more people here, two strangers in full walking gear, who have recognised me and want to know if I am Simon Armitage the poet. 'Yes,' I say. Because I am. I am Simon Armitage, lost but now found, sad but now happy and absolutely confident of my name and purpose. And because they sense that I am somewhat delirious and likely to agree to anything, they ask me if I will come and give a reading in a pub in Harrogate, and because I am ecstatic and elated and in love with everybody in the world who is not a cairn or a cloud, I say yes. Richard and his dog go off with the Harrogate contingent, and now I am walking with the runners, who can't help breaking out into a sprint here or a scamper there, which must be infectious because suddenly I'm putting in little surges of pace as well, the adrenalin and euphoria carrying me over Little Dun Fell, then past the eerie 'golf ball' aviation station on Great Dun Fell and across a metalled road onto another moor. It's still misty, still raining, but the runners don't seem to need any kind of navigational equipment, and their dogs go leaping and tumbling through the tuft grass and across the peat hags, and so do they. We stop for something to eat but I don't manage much food because I'm too busy gushing and babbling and running away at the mouth with all the excitement of an escapee. God knows what I tell them, or what they tell me that gets drowned out under my own stream of verbiage. The descent from Knock Fell and the house-shaped cairn of Knock Old Man is rapid, five hundred feet of altitude being lost in what seems like minutes, the finishing post not far away now, the conical and comical protuberances of Dufton Pike and Knock Pike providing a natural gateway into the appropriately tranquil Eden Valley. On the old clapper bridge over Great Rundale Beck I force Mars Bars on each of the fell-runners, draw breath and shut up for a while. Alastair, Andrew, Hester and Claire, aka Freckle, are not only my rescuers but poets themselves and organisers of tonight's reading. In a few hours' time they will emerge from tents round the back of Dufton Village Hall and I won't recognise them at first, no longer caked in mud or plastered with rain but miraculously transformed into clean, beautiful people, welcoming the audience at the door, checking tickets and running the little book stall and the makeshift bar. But they'll recognise me. I might have spent an hour steeping in one of Mrs Kindleysides' ornate baths, soaking up the products, scrubbing my nails, shampooing my hair, and I might have shaved and cleaned my teeth and applied lip balm, and I might now be swaggering towards the microphone in a smart jacket and ironed shirt, with a book of poems in my hand and a few one-liners up my sleeve. But they saw the gibbering ninny who came off that hill today, the expression on his face, the look in his eye, and it won't wash. Who am I trying to kid?

Dufton to Langdon Beck

12 MILES

OS Explorer OL19 North Sheet, OL31 West

Friday 16 July

At the end of last night's reading a man called Brian approached me and said, 'So where are you heading tomorrow, like?'

'To Langdon Beck,' I told him.

'I've done that walk a few times. Need some company?'

'The more the merrier.'

'Right,' said Brian. 'But I'm a bit of a fair-weather walker, like, so . . .'

And as an indication of today's weather forecast, suffice it to say that I am not expecting to see him. But Brian is standing under a tree in the rain with two other men, gathered around a cigarette belonging to my friend Rick, who has given up smoking, and must have left Huddersfield at an ungodly hour to get through the morning traffic and arrive in Dufton by 8 a.m. The other spectral figure, with water dripping from the rim of his hat, is Chris Woodley-Stewart, director of the North Pennines Area of Outstanding Natural Beauty (AONB) Partnership. This is his patch, and he's very kindly offered to guide me across it pointing out outstandingly beautiful natural features and highlighting AONB concerns along the way. He's also a bit of a poetry fan. He certainly reads it, from what he knows about Larkin and Hughes. He even quotes some of my own work, and if that's meant to impress me, it works. And like most people who read poetry I suspect Chris writes it as well, though I'm always careful not to ask.

The Pennine Way follows the proper road out of Dufton then veers left at Billysbeck Bridge and indeed runs parallel with Billy's Beck along a farm track towards Bow Hall. It feels unnatural to be turning due east when the whole point of the journey is to make my way south, and even more counterintuitive when the path starts angling north. In fact the whole of today's section describes a massive dog-leg, a reminder, if one were needed, that the Way is an artificially engineered trail rather than the retracing of some purposeful trade route from an age when travel through these hills was difficult and expensive and when leisure had not yet been invented. So no matter how much the course of the Eden Valley offers an easy and obvious way ahead, the rule book says that we must decline the invitation of the line of least resistance, me, Rick, Brian and Chris, and climb again through the contours, isotherms and isobars, into the clouds.

Like just about everyone with a thorough knowledge of this area, Chris's starting point seems to be geology, the bedrock which ultimately gives shape, structure and meaning to the territory we walk through. Even as a geography graduate I have to admit that not only have the finer points of geology eluded me, so too have most of its general principles. Either the time periods are too enormous to contemplate, or the processes too convoluted to understand, or the names too long to remember. I often equate it, at some unconscious, synaesthetic level, with the system used to acknowledge and celebrate wedding anniversaries, a system involving a hierarchy of naturally occurring minerals and one that spans less than a century, and since I can't remember that ten years is a tin wedding and forty is ruby, then I'm unlikely to remember what happened several million years ago and which particular stone it produced. Rocks, I'm happy to understand, are very old and very hard, and as long as they support my weight and don't move around too much, like they do in Iceland and other untrustworthy portions of the planet's crust, I'm quite content with that level of ignorance. Chris, though, reads the landscape vertically, from the bottom up. Every hundred yards or so he points out what to my eyes is an undetectable variation in the texture of the stone or the formation of an outcrop, and I admire anyone who can animate and give character to what on the face of it is the world's most inert and lifeless substance. Stopping to appreciate a high and long dry-stone wall that bisects two valleys, Chris explains how the shape, size, colour and consistency of the stones begins to change along its course, a consequence of wall-builders using the nearest available material while quarrying across a fault-line, so the wall becomes a kind of cross-section of the bedrock below us, and a timeline also, and after a few minutes of looking I almost convince myself that I can see the difference.

The Whin Sill is still the dominating geological subtext here, the massive volcanic plateau I first encountered at Hadrian's Wall, its exposed northern edge forming a dramatic stone palisade across the Northumbrian fells, whose eastern reaches promise an even more spectacular natural phenomenon if the guide books are to be trusted, something that has to be seen to be believed. In fact the only reason the Pennine Way makes such an inconvenient detour as it does today is to take in what some have referred to as the 'Grand Canyon of England'. High Cup Gill is a U-shaped chasm scooped from the earth by ice, the glacial action exposing breathtaking, almost architectural dolerite columns towards its top end, leaving epaulettes of the same volcanic rock along its flanks, especially along High Cup Scar on the south side, opposite the path, and creating the magnificent high-altitude waterfall of High Cup Nick at its head. Along with Malham Cove it is probably the most eagerly anticipated and frequently photographed landmark on the trail, a cover image for at least two trail guides, and one of those places which make the whole enterprise *worth it*. I've never been to High Cup before or anywhere close, but the internet bulges with images of its sweeping, elongated emptiness and its giant, intricate rock formations, and I've been looking forward to this day more than most, perhaps more than any. I'm excited about seeing a great big nothing, because for several days I've been staring at great big somethings in the shape of hills and mountains, and I'm hoping for a kind of clarifying and cleansing experience, a much needed obverse to yesterday's tangle with the brooding hulk that was Cross Fell, although unless the clouds lift I won't see anything at all. We have turned off a drove road and ascended a hill pockmarked with old mine workings and disused quarries, and are now fording several roaring streams, every one of them bursting and bubbling with brown water the colour of mild ale or porter, and edged with a creamy-looking froth to complete the beer analogy. The walker following the orthodox direction of the Pennine Way would approach High Cup from the north-east; in fact the trail is designed to maximise the effect, a gradual upstream trek alongside Maize Beck leading to a slow plod across the wet moor, then the sudden vista, and out come the cameras. Walking *up* the Gill, as we are, means the impression should be incremental rather than spontaneous, and even though visibility isn't more than about twenty yards, after another half-hour or so of climbing I sense a space opening up to my right, the presence of a void or hollowness, becoming deeper and more profound as we gain height and scramble up the mountain pass which the map refers to as Narrow Gate. This might have been an old packhorse route but I certainly wouldn't want to be up here on any kind of quadruped, having to trust its balance across the wet rocks and sections of slimy green grass. In truth I don't have too much confidence in my own footwork either, and find myself leaning noticeably away from the edge, crouching a little, favouring the left bank and stiffening my right leg as a prop against the overhang, even though there's no overhang to see. At Nichol Chair there's just enough visibility to make out the basalt column which a cobbler from Dufton supposedly once climbed, and while sitting on the top proceeded to mend a pair of shoes. Is he, I wonder, the Cumbrian version of Simeon Stylites, or St Simeon the Stylite, the son of a shepherd, who from an early age sought spiritual fulfilment through many forms of physical austerity? Before he was sixteen, Simeon began a fast from which he eventually had to be rescued, and could well be credited as the inventor of the gastric band, having tied a restrictive girdle of palm fronds so tightly around his stomach that the fibres had to be surgically removed from his flesh. He then spent a year or so without sitting down, then another year or so in a hut, followed by a period living in a narrow fissure in a rock face, which he eventually abandoned because of visiting pilgrims and rubberneckers. Finally he found himself a stone pillar in a ruined building, climbed up and stayed there for the next thirty-seven years, an achievement unlikely to be outdone, although I note with some disappointment that for all his effort he has never been officially recognised in the *Guinness Book of World Records*. Neither is there an entry for the fastest traverse of the Pennine Way, a record currently held, according to the internet, by one Mike Hartley, who covered the distance in two days, seventeen hours, twenty minutes and seventeen seconds, stopping for fish and chips in Alston and completing the last forty miles in a borrowed shoe which was two sizes too big. I also heard a rumour in one of the pubs that a blind Chinese man had run the Pennine Way in not much more than three or four days, a feat which I cannot begin to contemplate, especially when walking along the edge of High Cup Gill. Nichol Chair also brings to mind a scene in the seventies action thriller *The Eiger Sanction*, starring Clint Eastwood as an art-collecting, mountain-climbing assassin and George Kennedy as his double-crossing mentor and 'ground-man'. Training in the Arizona desert, Eastwood and Kennedy climb an extraordinary pinnacle or stack, one of those isolated fingers of stone which protrude vertically out of the sand and look ready to collapse at any moment, and while sitting on the summit Kennedy says that he could murder a can of beer. Eastwood replies something like, 'Who'd be mad enough to haul beer up here?' and Kennedy says, 'You would,' fishing two cans out of Eastwood's rucksack. None of us has been mad enough to haul beer up High Cup Nick, but we do have flasks, and we stand above the cleft in the rock where the stream plummets over the edge then comes flying back into our faces when the updraught gets underneath it. Then suddenly, in a moment of grace, the wind stirs the cloud and the mist parts, and just for a few seconds the whole of the valley is visible, the silver thread of the stream in the middle and the graphite-coloured path running alongside, the boulders and rocks littering the bottom, the sheer swooping descent of the valley sides, some of it grassed, some of it steep grey scree, the occupying ranks of tall, black, columnar stone along its upper border, but more than anything the sweeping majesty of its height and breadth and length, a dizzying vastness full to the brink with nothing but light and air. It seems too enormous and intangible to be caught on camera, so I try to experience it rather than capture it, memorise it as a sensation rather than a sight, by the only method that seems to make sense at the time: by breathing it in. Then the curtains close.

There's a frog splashing around in the spray from the waterfall, and some fairly nonchalant sheep, indifferent to both the view and the dangerous drop, but no sign of the peregrine falcons or ravens that make this habitat their home. The area directly behind the Nick is a flat, grassy no-man's land, not heath or hill or moor but an undecided, becalmed transition between the booming gravity of the Gill and the lumpy, swampy fell to follow. Between pulls on his cigarette, Water Drainage Manager Rick argues that a few linear miles of concrete channelling wouldn't go amiss up here, but also concedes that God or whoever has done a pretty decent job of sorting out the irrigation issues. Because this is a true watershed, the type we might imagine and hope for, where one watercourse very visibly makes its way over the lip of the falls, and another trickles very visibly in the direction of Maize Beck, which we find and follow, and which surprises me with its size and volume. A beck, in my book, is a stream, a classification based on the waterway that gurgled along the back of my auntie's house on Palace Avenue in Bridlington, never more than a couple of foot deep and four or five foot wide, ideal for damming with bricks and fallen branches, and always referred to as 'the beck'. Surely Maize Beck is a river, long, wide, fast and proud, with its threats of deluge and promise of trout. A few years ago it swelled so much it took out the bridge near Dobson Mere Foot, the only crossing point, and regularly floods to such an extent that an alternative route to the north has to be taken. What else must a watercourse do to prove itself not beck but river? Just before we reach the new bridge, Chris stops and nods in the direction of something murky and tall in the mist about thirty yards away, which at first glance looks to me like a very big, solidly built man in black clothes, a miner, or the ghost of a miner, a revenant. But it's a horse. They call them ponies here, fell ponies, but they also call a river a beck, and this is most definitely a horse in my dictionary, and so are the other four that materialise and dematerialise as the mist thins and thickens.

The area to the south is MOD land and there are signs warning against trespass, though no evidence of shelling or artillery fire today. After rounding the lower reaches of Meldon Hill the path begins to descend and the weather starts to improve. Chris says that the scarring on the far hills is where land-owners have mechanically cropped the heather so that grouse can feed on the young shoots. The tracts are unsightly, an unwitting form of graffiti without pattern or shape on the wide open canvas of the moor. I'd often wondered about those peculiar markings, and hoped they had a higher purpose than supplying forage for red grouse, birds introduced to the moor each year for no other reason than to provide target practice for shooters. Now I know different. And just for a few miles the notion of walking freely across the nation's wild and untamed regions is crowded out by thoughts of government intervention and private enterprise, or a feeling that this stretch of the Pennine Way is little more than a rat run between military bombardment on one side and gratuitous field sport on the other. The thinner lines which zigzag the landscape are vehicle tracks, laid down by 4x4s, allowing shooters to be driven right to the kill-site rather than stalk their prey and earn their trophies. When we shelter under a bank of crumbling black earth, it's like hunkering down in a trench, out of the firing line, though the sense of natural and ancient history is restored when Chris points out a silver birch twig protruding from a lower layer of peat, perfectly preserved for many millions of years. It's hard to imagine, but like so many desolate uplands in Britain this treeless and exposed plateau was once a wood. And as if it flies the flag or carries the candle for that particular idea, a lone sycamore stands outside the remote and lonely Birkdale Farm, sometimes said to be the highest occupied farmhouse in England, a somewhat convoluted and unwelcome distinction to my mind, like being the world's most southerly polar bear-watching station, or Britain's fattest potholer. Birkdale is a useful bearing on the wet slog between Moss Shop, a ruined mine, and the hideous concrete slab of Cow Green Dam, holding back some four hundred million gallons of water. Cow Green Reservoir was constructed between 1967 and

1971 at great expense and amid furious controversy. Conceived to supply the needs of the great manufacturing industries of the north-east, the project involved the flooding of a sensitive and unique 'alpine' environment, home to rare plants with a continuous history of survival dating back to the last ice age, including spring gentian, the Teesdale violet and several species of orchid. The famously bearded naturalist David Bellamy was one of many who lent his voice to a chorus of disapproval when the reservoir was first proposed, and although some good came from the project inasmuch as the surrounding land was designated a nature reserve, the large body of water which now fills the valley has something of a redundant reputation, the furnaces of industry down on the coast no longer building up anything like the same thirst these days, kettles and water coolers in open-plan call centres not generating quite the same demand. Whether by design or coincidence, the actual reservoir never becomes visible from the Pennine Way, the path cutting below the waterline in front of the dam wall and the car park before becoming a serious scramble down the fantastically named Cauldron Snout waterfall with the equally fantastically named cliffs of Falcon Clints running high alongside. Water bounces vigorously over the tumbled, light-coloured rocks, though it isn't quite nature in full flow since the rate of discharge from the dam is electronically and presumably remotely controlled. Where Maize Beck is finally upgraded to the River Tees at what used to be the intersection of the counties of Durham, Yorkshire and Westmorland, I watch a dipper in the foaming water, and a grey wagtail on a boulder, and two sandpipers scuttling along the riverbank, and an obliging falcon over Falcon

Clints. The Pennine Way follows the north bank of the river, which becomes the west bank when the trail seems to want to steer back towards Scotland, and the path here is virtually indistinguishable from the littering of boulders that have either rolled from the slopes or been washed downstream. It's less like a walk and more like an archaeological assignment among flooded ruins, leading to wet feet and bruised ankles. The river truly rushes along here, not deep but fast and noisy, garrulous even across the bed of stones and around small islands formed of bulrushes and clotted reeds. In fact we are now picking our way through a ravine, a narrowing passage of steep and high-sided valley walls, the first place on this trip that would lend itself to a successful ambush. When the valley eventually fans out onto a flood plain where the weather is altogether kinder and calmer than it was just half an hour ago, we sit and eat, and a shaggy-looking tup comes right up to Rick and takes a cheese sandwich out of his hand. I was wrong about the beer; I hear the unmistakable sound of a ring-pull being torn backwards, and when I turn to look, Brian is downing a can of lager. He's also taken off his waterproof to reveal a Carlisle United strip. The rivers here might run to the east but his loyalties flow in the opposite direction, and the conversation turns from environmental issues in the north Pennines to football trivia, notably the subject of legendary Carlisle goalie Jimmy Glass who came lumbering upfield in the ninety-fifth minute of his side's must-win match against Plymouth Argyll and duly volleyed home the winner, sparking a pitch invasion, in which Brian took part. The last time I read anything about him was in one of those 'where are they now' pieces, which found our hero now driving a taxi in Dorset, though his upbeat manner and positive attitude provoked the perhaps inevitable comment that 'for Jimmy the Glass will always be half full'.

It's about three in the afternoon when we reach the pub, via a small field with a 'BULL IN FIELD' sign pinned to the fence. About forty yards away, a very large bull-shaped creature is standing with its back to us, and there are no obvious escape routes other than the gate at the far end. There's also another sign offering advice to anyone confronted by bulls, most of which revolves around keeping the dog on a short leash or letting the dog go, and since we don't have a dog, tiptoeing seems to be our best option. Not many people are killed by cattle each year but some are, usually trampled, including a woman walking on the Pennine Way in 2009, and she was a vet. Before we cross the partly submerged Saur Hill Bridge we pass two men walking in the opposite direction, and all agree we wouldn't want to be hiking back up towards High Cup at this time in the late afternoon, with no prospect of accommodation or even shelter until Dufton. We also pass a farmer in his yard, power-washing a donkey with a high-pressure hose.

*

The *Odyssey* is one of the greatest works of western literature, and also one of the earliest, a sort of bedrock or foundation on which many subsequent stories are built. In what could also be described as one of the first pieces of travel writing, the *Odyssey* is presented as a poem, told by Homer, who may or may not have existed, and tells the tale of Odysseus's exhausting and beleaguered return from battle. Having

fought at Troy for ten years, and having finally brought the siege to an end via his cunning wooden-horse ruse, Odysseus sets sail for Ithaca. But the journey will take him another decade, during which time he outwits the Cyclops, is spellbound by the Sirens, sees his crew turned into pigs by the enchantress Circe, is kept as a love-slave by the goddess Calypso, meets the ghost of his mother in the underworld, and undergoes many more trials, tribulations and humiliations along the way. The poem is a ten-year homecoming, and there are few more touching scenes than when Odysseus falls asleep while being transported over the sea to his own island, and wakes up alone on the beach, not recognising his kingdom, just a few miles from his palace but still lost in his mind. When he left Ithaca to fight the Trojans, his son Telemachus was just a babe in arms; now he is a young man with a beard. As Odysseus approaches his palace, disguised as a beggar, he sees his old hunting hound, Argos, blind and lying on a bed of dung, still pining for his master after all these years. Sensing Odysseus's presence, the dog rallies for a brief moment, then his heart fails. Finally, after slaying all the suitors who have laid siege to his kingdom and his wife, Odysseus is reunited with Penelope, and they retire to the famous marital bed, made from the bole of a living olive tree, around which the whole chamber is constructed.

In front of the bay window of the Langdon Beck Hotel I read that section from the poem. There's a big crowd – it's almost certainly the biggest poetry reading taking place in Upper Teesdale this weekend – with rows of people all the way back as far as the bar, some leaning in through open doors, others propped in alcoves, and through the glass behind me a line of parked cars on the single-track road stretches away into the evening. But I read this piece for my wife and my daughter, sitting on two small bar stools in the middle distance of the pub. Then we eat together, not quite a candlelit meal but a quiet, private occasion all the same, then go to the room, where one single camp bed is positioned alongside one double bed, like a lifeboat tethered to a yacht, and for a while we whisper in the dark, and giggle a few times, then whisper some more, then fall asleep. And I dream of horses.

Fell Ponies

They have got up
out of the dirt, the first
hauling the buried boat or ramshackle cart
of its own self

from a ditch.
Then four more follow,
the props of their legs
fossilised limbs of oak,

because there were forests here once.
Not ponies as we know them
but big-engined,
an early design,

leather straps and hardwood cogs
at work when they move,
boulders for ballast
swinging in rope sacks

strung from a crude frame,
the flesh
an all-over daub
of soil and mulch that won't set.

But a lean burn all the same –
just enough breath
on the oil
to keep the lamp in flame . . .

All this gone wild,
Ashington escapees grown moody and mean
on aloneness and sleet.
They trundle forward

into some old war, then forget,
or blink awake from a dream
of pack road or pit,
of ploughs or sleds

at their heels,
then lower their heads
to browse on root and weed.
Wherever they halt

is the world's edge,
or they wait
just an inch from the future's wall of glass,
seeing nothing,

taking it all in, at any moment
to turn into mist, or re-emerge,
come lumbering
out of the flooded mine,

now cut-outs up on the ridge,
now barring the path to the bridge,
seaweed fringes and axe-head stares,
their hides

knotted rugs of rags
slung over the beam of the spine,
all smoke and steam,
ignited by lightning strike in the first storm,

put out by rain.

Langdon Beck to Baldersdale

15 MILES

OS Explorer OL31 West Sheet, OL19 North, OL31 East

Saturday 17 July

My daughter says, 'This is a funny holiday.' Last night she toured around the audience with the begging sock, and this morning she has tipped out the proceeds and counted the coins and notes into piles and wads, and arranged them on the windowsill, next to my boots which are overflowing with soggy, scrunched-up balls of yesterday's *Guardian* and above several pairs of socks steaming on the radiator. In my notebook she calculates that the £207 handed over by the fifty-five-strong audience works out at £3.763636363 recurring per person, and when I tell her that I counted fifty-seven people sitting in front of me last night she says, 'Yes, but me and Mummy didn't pay.' In her neat, exaggerated A-is-for-apple handwriting she has also recorded several other items that found their way into the sock, including one Refresher chew, one magazine photograph of a dipper with the words 'Watch out for dippers' written below it, one HP Sauce sachet, two biros, one lavender bag, one page of the *Daily Telegraph* folded into a small square (with no news items relevant to my project, as far as I can tell), one poem entitled 'Ten Things Mark Rothko Told Me', and one pair of silver cufflinks. As a walker on the Pennine Way I think I could probably find a use for most of those items (especially the page from the *Telegraph*, in an emergency), with the exception of the cufflinks, which on reflection seem like a cruel jibe.

*

Today's walk, or at least the first half of it, is reckoned by many to be the most pleasant and least taxing section of the whole trail, a saunter through pretty Teesdale along the banks of the Tees, with no route-finding difficulties whatsoever and several picturesque and iconic landmarks to tick off along the way. That's a relief, given that I'm still reeling from what happened on Cross Fell. On the other hand it's going to give my wife and daughter, walking with me today, the impression that for the last nine days I've done nothing more than wander through buttercup meadows from one public house to the next, making friends and showing off along the way and being paid for the privilege. To counter that notion, I go through an elaborate per-formance before breakfast, pulling heaps of filthy clothes from the Tombstone, describing to my wife how and where each garment came to be blackened, bloodied or saturated, and giving a mile-by-mile, blow-by-blow account of my most hair-raising experiences thus far. But she pulls back the curtains and the sun is blazing across the valley, and in a T-shirt and trainers she waits for me in the car park while I tie the very long laces of my very big boots and secure all toggles and zips. My daughter has also taken the casual rather than cautious approach, and strides out ahead of us in pink leggings, white iPod earphones, a pair of canvas shoes that are not far from being slippers, and a vest. Her coat, which she wears tied around her waist, was given to her by a man called Charles in a pub car park in West Yorkshire, who also gave me several items of clothing made entirely from organic, natural fibres to 'trial' during my walk, including a very nice fleece, a luminous orange anorak and a top made out of recycled wood chippings. The exchange, even though it had been pre-arranged and was all above board, must have looked very suspicious from the street, with two cars pulling up boot to boot, two strangers shaking hands, one man producing a range of clothes from the back of his car while the other man and his daughter tried them on, followed by another handshake and the vehicles shooting off in opposite directions. Even though she wears it around her middle rather than in the prescribed manner, my daughter was particularly thrilled with her acquisition when she learned that it was 'bombproof'. Army green and slightly sinister-looking, it's made from a fabric called Ventile, developed in the Second World War for pilots at risk of being shot down over the sea. When it becomes wet the cotton in it expands, making it waterproof, apparently. It is also windproof and much coveted by 'bushcraft' people who need to sneak up on birds and animals, because it doesn't rustle. Modelling it in the car park outside the Co-op that day, my daughter had the look of a special forces trainee, and responded to that suggestion by giving me a highly convincing karate kick between the legs (and while I was getting my breath back, a punch in the kidneys).

We're not expecting bombshells today, or even rain. The first stretch of the path loops up and over a set of crags with juniper bushes to each side, then down a grassy embankment before rejoining the river. My daughter might be out in front, proving that no map is necessary, but we're actually following Shane Harris, a colleague of Chris's from North Pennines AONB, and his wife, Cath. The juniper is a particular and peculiar feature of this area, Shane explains, and as we brush

past the spiky leaves I convince myself I can smell gin. With their knotted, wrenched trunks and bleached, desiccated branches, the junipers are reminiscent of wild olive trees, giving the immediate landscape a biblical feel, as if we're walking though the Holy Land, an atmosphere which lasts until the appearance of Dine Holm quarry and stone-cutting plant on the left-hand side, which explains the fine yellowy powder coating the shrubs, the grass and eventually our feet. Less than quarter of an hour later we're standing above High Force, silent as we approached it from upstream, but now a roaring, drumming volley of white water hurling itself over a cliff face and thundering into the deep pool seventy or so feet below. Standing on the ridge above, I can feel the pulsing power of the water in the soles of my feet and my solar plexus, and there's an even better view thirty yards downstream, looking back at the full spectacle of the falls from a stone outcrop which provides a natural viewing gallery and a photo opportunity. The noise of High Force is amplified by the semicircular gorge into which the river is delivered, a feature which also magnifies its visual appeal. It's so perfect it could have been designed, and those Darwinism-deniers who seem to be finding increasing employment opportunities in American schools might even argue it was. To keep my daughter away from the edge I've told her the legend of Peg Powler, a green-haired water hag who is said to inhabit this valley. Wherever she goes she leaves a frothy substance on the surface, known as Peg Powler's Suds, and she feeds on children, grabbing them by the ankle if they stray too close to the river.

We eventually move off without incident, which is a relief in the sense that the last time we visited a waterfall as a family we were arrested. It was in those tense few years following 9/11, and while working in Toronto we'd hired a car for a day trip to Niagara Falls. We arrived there just before lunch, and after an hour or so decided we'd like to look into the foaming abyss from the other shore, so without realising we were heading for the United States we set off across the bridge without our passports. This is something that probably happens twenty or thirty times a day, but rather than just turning us around and sending us back, the guard in the booth, with the gun and the sunglasses and the moustache, made us park up and sit down in the holding area with several dozen other unfortunates, where we waited for an hour and a half. If the atmosphere was meant to be intimidating, it worked. The uniformed officers shouted obscenities at one another and answered every question I put to them with, 'Take a seat.' I remember making eye contact with one officer who was holding an old-fashioned typewriter in his hands. After a few seconds he deliberately let it crash to the floor, but never stopped staring at me, even though my daughter had jumped on to my lap and started to sob. We were eventually 'interviewed' by another pair of sunglasses and moustache, then photographed, then fingerprinted, and after signing statements and admissions about our transgression were escorted back down to the pound, where the car had been searched and was standing with all four doors, bonnet and boot open, and the floor-mats scattered on the ground along with the spare wheel and the contents of the toolkit. They said we probably wouldn't be let back into Canada, suggesting we'd just have to live forever on the bridge, cadging fruit and peanuts from passing motorists and drinking the spray thrown up by the mighty falls, but the guard at the north end just smiled and waved us through.

*

Walking the Pennine Way in the traditional direction, Low Force waterfall would be experienced as a taster of bigger and better things to come, but approaching it after High Force it is, inevitably, something of a downgrade. All the way along the river, bridges reach out from one bank to the other, some fairly robust, others more flimsy and hopeful, hanging by stakes and pulleys, their suspensions more like suspensions of disbelief, Indiana Jones-style contraptions made of wires and hawsers, with swaying walkways spanning the swirling eddies and rapids below. The path on the riverbank is a natural arched colonnade, a cloistered alleyway beneath overhanging alder, willow, hazel, birch and rowan, with rafts of meadowsweet lining the verges and poppies growing out of cracks in the damp stone wall. My wife says that the humidity and the smell of wild flowers recalls her trekking days in the Himalayas, a smiling reminder that by comparison my own journey is a mere stroll in the garden. The narrow path necessitates walking in single file, meaning that most conversations are conducted over the shoulder or towards the back of someone's neck. Despite which, I manage to talk to Shane about a shared interest, Rackwick, on the island of Hoy. To the Orkney poet George Mackay Brown, whose entire poetic universe didn't extend much further than the view from his window and the graveyard at the end of the road, Rackwick became a sacred location, a depopulated valley and dramatic bay which opened its arms to the blast of the Atlantic, full of ghosts, legends, stories and poems. The trip to Rackwick, usually hitched on a fishing boat or passing ferry, became a kind of pilgrimage to Mackay Brown, a challenge to his permanently frail health but a source of nourishment for his soul and his writing. Standing there with the gold flakes of his TB injection tumbling through his bloodstream, I think he saw something of Eden in Rackwick, the long grassed valley where the hull of a glacier had once berthed between two barren summits. Like Mackay Brown, I believe completely in Rackwick as a place of wonder and glory, a holy poetic location, but unlike him I have never been there, my experience of it being entirely vicarious, firstly through his poems and prose, then through days looking at maps and staring at satellite images on Google Earth, imagining myself wandering across the sand in bare feet or bunking up for the night in a deserted croft set back from the ocean. I can't remember how we get onto the subject, but when we do it turns out that Shane has not only been to Hoy but spent many days conducting research at Rackwick, and once I know this, I instantly promote him from AONB Communications Officer to messenger of the gods.

'What were you doing there?'

'I was measuring rocks, to find out if they were bigger at one side of the bay than the other.'

We walk on for another five minutes in silence, while I ponder Shane with his tape measure or micrometer, scrambling around on the shoreline of Rackwick for lonely but blissful days at a time, scrutinising the same stones that lined the boundary and marked the gateway of Mackay Brown's world, stones that shone and wept and sang in the poet's imagination, before I say, 'And what was the conclusion?'

'Yes,' Shane says, 'they were.'

Once, at the Santuari de Lluc in north-west Mallorca, I peeled off from a guided tour of the Stations of the Cross, situated along a stepped path which spiralled towards the summit of the hill, and peered over a wall looking inland, away from the monastery and the gift shop, towards the mountains. Much of that part of Mallorca is dusty and somewhat drab, but the bowl of the valley which opened up beneath me was completely green, and ringed with terraced walls, all lined with pomegranate and lemon trees, the fruit hanging like lamps. Down in the bottom of the valley there were three or four fincas and three or four fields of pasture, with wooden gates set into the stone walls. It was an idealised scene, incongruous and unexpected. There were no visible roads in or out of the valley, so it gave the impression of a place trapped under glass, held in a bubble of space and time. Then a tractor appeared in one of the lower fields, and a farmer got out of the cab and tipped several bags of feed into a trough, and ran what looked like a hammer along the grille which covered it. The hammer clanged against the iron bars, and a few moments of silence followed. Then bells started to ring. Not church bells but small, tinny-sounding bells, like the noise made by those candle-driven, rotating angels on a Christmas decoration, pinging a cymbal with a wand as they sail past. Or small coins thrown in a metal cup. Rain in a pan. Then more bells making the same sound, then dozens, then hundreds, so the whole dome of the valley was quickly filled with that strange chiming, and on the far hillside I saw what I thought was a stream of light brown water pouring through a rocky channel, then another stream, and more streams here and there tumbling from the horizon through stands of olive trees and across walled terraces, until the whole crucible appeared to be in flood, with torrents flowing downhill from every side and from all angles, all heading for the flat fields in the bottom, and not until they streamed towards the feeding troughs could I see that they were rivers of goats, thousands of tan-coloured goats and kids with bells around their necks, jumping and pushing, barging and jostling as they raced towards the food. And new lines and columns of goats emerged out of the groves and crags, came spilling out of the woods or funnelling through an open gate, pouring and pouring from the hills, until the vale in the bottom was overtaken with a swirling lake of brown goats, and the whole of the valley was itself a bell, ringing and ringing, sounding their appearance, announcing mass.

*

I watch my wife and daughter waving from the back window of a small country bus as it trundles along the main road out of Middleton-in-Teesdale towards vanishing point, heading for the Langdon Beck Hotel. They have to leave now, go home to a world of work and school, promising to come and see me again sometime soon but without being able to say where or when. Feeling a bit sorry for myself I try to summon up interest in an ornate drinking fountain in the Horse Market, a leafy, cast-iron arrangement with columns and a domed black roof harbouring a white child sitting in a washbasin on a pedestal. From what I can gather, it seems to have been presented to one Chief Officer Bainbridge of the London Lead Company by his company employees, in what strikes me as a perverse or at least old-fashioned act of forelock-tugging. Then I wander across the road and take some photographs of an off-licence and general store by the name of Armitage, which, because that happens to be my name, is humorous. The business is up for sale, and Shane points out that if I were to buy it I would be spared the expense of a new sign. A few doors along there's a double-fronted shop called J. E. & V. Winter selling fishing jackets, thermos flasks and all kinds of outdoor gear, and because I'm a walker I go in. It's one of those shops with sheets of coloured gel at the window, giving everything inside a slight tinge of sepia and a slight sense of yesteryear. I poke around in a bucket of slippers

and try on a hat, then see a stook of walking sticks propped in a corner with the umbrellas, some antiquated models with the heads of dogs and horses etc. carved into the handles, but also a range of lightweight, retractable aluminium poles.

'I had a pair of these but I left them in Kielder Forest,' I tell the lady in the shop, who has appeared from nowhere, down some steps perhaps or out of a back room, and is suddenly standing behind me.

'What do you think of that one?' she says.

'Very nice,' I tell her, putting my weight on it, then doing a rather ridiculous lap of the shop, then holding it out along my line of sight, as if inspecting a fishing rod or a hunting rifle.

'Take it,' she says.

'What do you mean?'

'Take it if you like it. You can have it.'

For all their stock, J. E. & V. Winter's don't exactly appear to be doing a roaring trade, and I can't understand why I'm being given something for free. Then the lady says, 'I know who you are and I know what you're doing, and I think it's great. So if you want it, it's yours.' And we stand there for a few moments, among the boxes of sensible shoes, the rotary display of woollen socks, the pigeon holes of carefully folded knitted cardigans and rails of fleeces and plastic cagoules, and the traffic goes past outside. All along this journey people have given me their time, their money, the benefit of their experience and the full range of their hospitality, but on every occasion it's been part of an agreed barter, a trade, even if I've only given them a few words in exchange. But this is an act of pure kindness, unbidden, with nothing expected in return, and comes not from a position of affordable generosity but from a gentle heart in a quiet shop in an ordinary town.

'Only if I can send you a book,' I say, which I realise as soon as I've said it sounds horribly conditional and self-regarding, as if I'll only take the stick if she agrees to read my poems. She smiles and shrugs, then comes to the door to see me off down the street, marching with a spring in my step past the selection of seasonal vegetables in the boxes outside Armitage's and jabbing the pavement with the rubberised tip of my new pole.

*

It's just me and Shane now, leaving the easy, downhill gradient of the Tees to go south across the grain of the valleys, to rise and fall through Lunedale then Baldersdale, the path like a tightrope between reservoirs and dams, the thighs burning and the heart pumping for the first time all day. When we've gained height we turn and look down on the hundreds of white farmhouses dotted across the landscape, luminous in the afternoon sun. All the properties belonging to a previous landowning Lord Barnard were painted that colour at his insistence, it is said, and there are several versions of a local anecdote to explain his reasoning, some involving a broken leg and a horse. Shane points out the many hay meadows, pastureland that dairy farmers have given over to native grasses and wild flowers though a combination of persuasive argument and financial incentive. Over the years the hay meadows have become a striking feature of this region, not just providing a haven for rare and endangered species of flora and a habitat for wildlife, but also lending colour and texture to the landscape. The meadows are still mown for winter fodder, and it's even argued by some that the dolly mixture of mixed petals and leaves provides a healthier diet than the same acreage of your bog-standard green grass, or certainly a tastier one. We sit down in the middle of one of the meadows, with Melancholy Thistle and Yellow Rattle, also known as Poverty, forming a fringed and swaying horizon in front of our eyes, with the blank wall of Selset Reservoir beyond, and beyond that, the open wounds of new quarries and the closed sockets and half-healed scars of old ones. Before we reach Blackton, the end of today's walk, we pass through Hannah's Meadow, and even make a voluntary detour along a pontoon of duckboarding to Hannah's Barn, a museum and exhibition space dedicated

to the life and times of Hannah Hauxwell, the no-nonsense spinster made famous in the seventies through a series of TV documentaries depicting her unremittingly tough life on a northern hill farm. All I remember of the programmes are endless shots of Hannah with a bucket in her hand struggling against driving winds and lashing rain, or Hannah sitting in front of a meagre fire in a miserable-looking front room, and somewhere along the line I have confused or perhaps conflated an image of Hannah with an image of Mother Teresa. The barn, when we lift the latch and go inside, seems like the perfect shrine, inasmuch as it is completely empty.

Dark clouds are moving in as we arrive at Blackton Grange, once a youth hostel, now a 'truly unique training and development centre', and I'm just beginning to wonder if the chain of contacts has broken down when the silhouette of a serious-looking, Politburo-black 4x4 crosses the dam wall of Balderhead Reservoir, and behind tinted windows I'm voluntarily *renditioned* by Peter and Jane in an easterly direction, I think, judging by the sun, or maybe northwards. I don't really know where I'm being taken and to be honest I don't really care, because the seats are leather, the suspension smooth and the air conditioning is set at an unwavering twenty-two degrees. I'm not walking, I'm not outside, and the white lines down the middle of the road go past with a hypnotic regularity perhaps for an hour or so, till the gates of a large, modernised ranch-style property swing open, and upstairs, in the guest suite, the water is hot and the bath deep.

Peter was in pharmaceuticals and is now a farmer, albeit a very tidy and considerate one, and his estate is a veritable

Southfork in comparison with many of the dilapidated and ramshackle farms I've been stealing through or walking around in the north Pennines. In a pair of Peter's wellies I follow him across paddocks and orchards, making a tour of the acres and inspecting some of the animals, many of which have names. From one hillside he calls across to another, and several cattle emerge out of the shrubs and trees, followed eventually by a black bull, bringing up the rear and pawing the ground. 'Come on then,' Peter shouts, then, 'Come on. Come on then,' and they do come, slowly at first, then with more enthusiasm and momentum, until hopping over a wooden gate and admiring them from behind an electric fence seems the smart thing to do. The bull watches us from the top of a dusty mound, still snorting and shaking his head, undisputed king of the hill. Further along we look in on a family of pigs, ears over their eyes, snouts in the soil, rootling and foraging in a sectioned-off area under a stand of trees, kept in by white tape strung between metal posts, presumably carrying a mild electric current. Pigs have a reputation for eating anything and everything, from kitchen slops to car parts to dead bodies, and judging by an enclosure on the other side of the path where they were previously penned, it would appear that their status as the ultimate omnivore is well deserved. Because what must have been a pleasant glade with decorative undergrowth until last month is now a scene of devastation, post-apocalyptic, nothing but dust and mud, the margins pock-marked with hoofprints, grubbing-holes and abandoned burrowings, the centre like a bombsite or crater flooded with a pool of dirty black water. Even the mud looks as if it has been bitten and chewed. There isn't a blade of grass or a scrap of nourishment left. In fact the only living thing is a single, ferocious-looking bramble, about ten foot long and as thick as a wrist, studded with dagger-like thorns, and Peter says the pigs would have happily eaten that as well given time, beginning with the roots. In another field, an aloof ram prefers his own thoughts to our company. The great curled conches of his horns twist around his head and ears and across his face; we call him, but all he can hear in those enormous shells, I imagine, is the sea.

This little pre-dinner turn around the grounds, even after a day's walk and even though I'm tired, is very welcome, partly because it's an aimless ramble rather than an organised route march, drawing on a completely different set of muscles and requiring a much more relaxed mindset, and partly because it buys me time to think about the evening ahead. I've given readings in some very peculiar places, sometimes to some very peculiar people, and by my own admission I have given some very peculiar performances and read some very peculiar poems. But the audience tonight is just six people – Peter and Jane plus two other couples. Not a public event at all but a kind of evening's entertainment provided by the houseguest. So after supper we file through to the living room, a long, high study in fact with a galleried library, and find places to sit among the chairs, settees and soft furnishings. Then I wait for a pause in the conversation before saying, 'OK. Right. Well. Er . . .'

It's fine. I've had three bottles of strong beer and three glasses of red wine, and that of course always makes things finer than they actually are. But it's fine. A bit like a house-church meeting, with me leading the prayers, and apart from the booze a bit like an AA meeting: Hello, I'm Simon, and I'm a poet. But it's fine. I avoid eye contact because I don't want to look like a desperate raconteur in search of a response, and I don't try to say anything funny in case no one laughs, and I don't read anything sad in case someone takes it personally, and I finish with a question to the 'audience' so it's more like a chat and less like THE END, which avoids the potential embarrassment of polite applause from six pairs of hands, or no applause at all, and I don't hand the sock around because somehow I feel that the people in the room have already paid just by BEING HERE and going along with it. And it's also fine because later on there's just enough mobile-phone signal somewhere near the pillow of my wide and deeply sprung bed to call home, and the last thing I remember saying to my wife before I fall asleep, when she asks what it was like, is that it was fine, fine, even if it was the first reading I've ever given without wearing shoes.

Yellow Rattle Poverty

Hairless, leaves unstalked, toothed.
Two-lipped, lower lip decurved.
Calyx distended in fruit. Semi-parasite,

throws itself on the parish,
gets its hooks into good roots.
A beggar to shift

once it gains a toe-hold.
Bad-mouthed by farm-folk.
Goes among meadows, grassy places.

Hard times, one by the verge,
hunched, cap in hand,
shaking the poor-box, the husk

of its see-through purse
in its see-through fingers,
dry-voiced, whispering

spare any change, sir,
a penny for Fiddlecase,
a penny for Shacklebasket,
penny for old Hayshackle, sir,
help poor Pots 'n' Pans,
a penny for Rattle Jack,
spare a few pence for old Pepperbox, sir,
a penny for Cockscomb,
a ha'penny for old Hen Penny, sir,
remember old Shepherd's Coffin,
remember poor Snaffles,
a penny for Poverty, sir, most kindly,

when I brush past,
when I breeze through,
when I swish by.

Baldersdale to Keld

14 MILES

OS Explorer OL 31 East Sheet, OL 30 North

Sunday 18 July

Despite the fact that a mound of suppurating dirty clothes and several hundred coins of the realm have been taken off to Yorkshire by my family, the Tombstone is still supernaturally heavy. Even Peter and Jane's all-terrain, all-weather, all-powerful vehicle seems to grunt and stoop under the weight when I clean-and-jerk it into the air then heave it into the boot. It must look like I've been stealing cutlery, or even furniture, or even large farm animals, but the real problem, as always, is books. In the next life, I'm coming back as a nanotechnologist.

Peter is walking with me, and so is Paul, who tells me he is a journalist, and has been parachuted into County Durham by a national newspaper to write a story about my journey. I've no idea if this is true (and no such piece ever appears in the paper, as far as I know) but telling a lie just to accompany a poet on a fourteen-mile slog across some of the wettest and bleakest moorland in the country would be like admitting to a crime you hadn't committed. He's done lots of travel reporting and is well kitted out, and so is Peter, with any number of electronic devices attached to his person for keeping tabs on our direction of travel and our rate of progress. In fact he's so well equipped and willing to claim the role of navigator that I don't even bother getting the map out, thinking I'll just take the opportunity to enjoy the scenery for a change and let the responsibility and the blame fall elsewhere. And the scenery, once we've climbed to the top of Cotherstone Moor, hurdling the ditches, bogs and 'sikes' running laterally across the track, is something to behold. Not because of any dramatic features or breathtaking panoramic vista, but simply because after days and days and miles and miles of trudging across mountain, hill and moor, I'd expected some kind of easing of the terrain, a falling away towards lowlands and dales and eventually the big populations of the north. But up ahead there is only more of what there was behind. More moor, more hill, more empty upland, layer after layer, row after row, horizon after horizon. I try to count the summits and the valley systems, but there are too many, all blurring and blending, some hazy in morning sun, others darkened by cloud-shadow and rain, others hung with low cloud, just an unending sequence of elongated whalebacks and high ground for as far as the eye can see, for as far as I need to walk and probably further still. Yesterday I felt as if I was getting somewhere. From the top of Race Yate Rigg I feel as if I have barely begun.

'One point eight miles,' says Peter.

Then 'One point nine,' a tenth of a mile further on, by which time we're heading downhill towards what we think might be the A66 but turns out to be a well-made vehicle track running alongside Deepdale Beck. There's a shooting hut, with boarded-up windows at shooting height, and just enough fibrous vegetation to justify a game of Pooh-sticks from the bridge, Paul 'the reporter' being a clear winner with his streamlined stalk of grass, a veritable speedboat compared with my stringy twig of dead heather which becomes becalmed in a bay to one side of the main channel and which I finally scuttle with a large clod of earth. The next stretch is over another barren elevation, populated by small cairns at regular intervals, like relics of a primitive religion or ritualistic practice, their form and function not yet fully understood. There are dozens of them, and dozens of red grouse too, whose numbers on this moor seem absurd, even to the point where they explode out from under our feet every ten yards or so or waddle off in family groups of seven or eight led by the mother, so many in fact that it would probably be harder to miss a grouse with a shotgun, even when firing blind drunk, than to hit one. I've heard it said that to create a diversion and allow her young to escape the female grouse will sometimes feign injury by dragging a wing and floundering along the ground, but I've never seen it, even though on these overstocked acres some of these birds are almost within grabbing distance.

The main road, when we do arrive, is incomprehensible to the Pennine Wayfarer. Most days, the fastest thing I've seen is a pheasant, and they only go for about a hundred yards before running out of puff. Suddenly I'm looking at car after car, metallic and pearlescent colours flashing past at sixty, seventy, eighty miles an hour, and juggernauts thundering along, and screaming motorbikes and rattling caravans. It feels more like crossfire than traffic, with the three of us in no-man's land stranded on the verge, contemplating a dash to the other side. But rather than force the switched-off, somnambulant hiker to run its gauntlet, the Pennine Way turns right then left into a purpose-built subway, another incongruous experience. Inside it, on the concrete wall, someone has drawn a vertical line with a black marker pen and written, 'Congratulations on reaching the half way point on the PW – good luck.' Underneath, someone has scratched the word 'Suckers'.

In the meadow on the far side I watch a deer vault over a deer-proof fence from a standing start, then cross God's Bridge in the valley bottom, an ancient arrangement of pillars and slabs not especially worthy of the Almighty, then gain height by walking straight up a rough field with a truly enormous bull wandering alongside us, albeit on the other side of a stone wall. As well as taking an interest in desirable residences and covetable properties on the trail, I've also been making a mental note of places that are truly ugly, and somewhere in the next valley I see my least favourite house so far, a dark, uninviting manor flanked by brutalist, breeze-block barns, surrounded on three sides by defunct agricultural machinery and on the fourth by a steep embankment strewn with household rubbish and blue plastic barrels. Shambolic and gloomy animals graze among the junk, including a joyless donkey, two weatherbeaten horses and a handful of dishcloth-coloured sheep. A dog sleeps on the roof of a wheelless and windowless tractor, and to complete the effect, a crow is perched on the off-kilter chimney pot. Out of which, smoke rises, meaning someone actually lives there, and I wonder what Peter makes of such a place, so squalid and desolate in comparison with his own tended and cherished acres. But when I turn around he's checking the miles and the minutes and the vectors and degrees, and has worked out that's it's probably time for lunch. A good time to refuel, in fact, before the assault on Tan Hill, and Paul's girlfriend has made some 'Kindness of

Strangers' buns which he is keen to share if only because it lightens his load. As with every day so far, I've no idea as to the contents of my lunch box until I open it, and today's lucky dip contains a slab of your actual Kendal Mint Cake, that legendary item of hiking folklore, almost as much a comedy prop as an actual foodstuff, utterly iconic and virtually inedible.

A mile or so after Jack Shields Bridge (Peter supplies a more accurate calculation) the track forks, and even though the left fork looks more inviting, the Pennine Way goes right, and the gradient increases, and the weather turns. As well as learning to read the lie of the land and the meaning of the clouds, another arcane skill I've developed on this walk is to determine the ground conditions ahead by studying the state of oncoming walkers, and on that front alone, the omens are not good. Two men with big walking packs on their backs are daubed in mud to well above their gaiters, and another solitary walker must have fallen in a peat bog, because one side of his body appears to have been dipped in tar and his face is splashed with dirty brown streaks. A woman in a yellow cape is sheltering under a bridge eating a sandwich, and when I ask her what it's like further on she just shakes her head, which is Pennine Way sign language for horrible. But before the swamp we have to deal with the wind, which is absolutely raging against us, and which is loaded with a fine vapour, not really rain, but stinging to the eyes and the skin, and at this air-speed, like being spray-painted. There must be something comical about the three of us trying to push forward into it, cheeks flattened with the G-force, coats ballooned with air, trousers vacuum-packed around our legs, hair streaming behind along with scarves and straps and anything else that isn't tied down or tucked in, but it's hard to see the funny side. It's even harder to say anything, the wind tearing off and shredding every utterance as it leaves the lips, and it's during long, gruelling, uphill passages like this, disadvantaged by every element, that I concede the Pennine Way really should be tackled from south to north, not north to south. It feels interminable, relentless, and there's no option but to keep pushing on. The weather, never less than interesting in these parts, is now excelling itself, and has gone into a sort of hyperactive, attention-seeking overdrive; mist, then a downpour, then a sudden blast of blinding sunlight from between two clouds with a rainbow thrown in for effect, then a thrashing squall accompanied by thunder, then dark cloud, and all of it hurried and harried and driven along by the blasting wind. We pass a series of sinister-looking shooting huts to the right, like gun emplacements, a reminder again that these moors are not the playgrounds of the commoner but owned, private land, managed and manip-ulated by interested parties for the purpose of profit. A stream runs to the left, and a series of white-painted posts marks the route for about a mile before petering out.

Possibly as a mental retreat from the misery of the situation I find myself making lists. First, a list of things I've lost on this walk, including my two poles, one compass, one zip-up fleece and one copy of my *Selected Poems*. To that list I also add half a stone in weight (a conservative estimate if the notches on my belt are anything to go by), some abstract concepts like my sense of humour, especially on occasions like this, and 'my way', twice, once in the Cheviots, once on Cross Fell. I then list my injuries: five horsefly bites, a bloody thumb, some soreness in the big toe of my right foot when bent backwards, windburn on my face, chapped lips, and the odd moment of wounded pride. But no blisters, which is both mystery and miracle combined. On we go, into it, at it, the Tan Hill Inn being our immediate objective. It appears at one moment, like a boat adrift on the horizon in a terrible storm, then slips below a hill, and half an hour later when we have climbed that hill we see it again, but further away somehow, even more remote, receding with every step. Unlike the wind, which has not receded at all but grown stronger with altitude, and walking into it is an enormous effort, reminiscent of hauling a great weight, something like a big sledge with rusty runners and an anchor trailing behind, and on that sledge my spirit, sulking and unwilling, not happy, heavy and unhelpful, facing backwards with its arms crossed and its bottom lip stuck out, heels dragging in the dirt.

I also have to question the extent to which the final ascent of Sleightholme Moor can legitimately be termed a 'path', when in all honesty it is a quagmire, half a mile of sticky toffee pudding and black treacle with just the odd tussock to leap for. The mud, when I stand in it, which is unavoidable, is reluctant to let go, and wants to rive off my boots and my trousers as well given half a chance, and I make several detours left and right looking for a land-bridge or something with grass on it, only to be blocked by either a swamp, a flooded ditch, a stream in full flow or one of those ghostly, rheumy ponds of standing water which in the film version of this escapade would be full of severed heads. Finally, having splashed off the moor on all fours, sodden and dripping and cold, I turn around and look back over the wet, shifting horizons and the heaving summits, and at the rain-filled valleys and swelling moors. More than anything else, it looks like the ocean.

*

Two cockerels are perched on the windowsill of the Tan Hill Inn, and a few more are strutting around in the car park. Just outside the door, blown over by the wind, an old woman on her back with her orange dress up around her head is being helped to her feet, and there is a sheep in the lobby. The Tan Hill, at 1,732 feet above sea level, claims to be Britain's highest pub, a claim disputed by the Cat and Fiddle Inn in the Peak District. Its fame and possibly its fortune as well were secured in the seventies through a series of adverts for Everest double glazing, in which celebrity farmer Ted Moult let a feather fall undisturbed through the air in front of one of the windows while a storm raged against the glass on the outside. The windows are still doing their job but I'm sad to learn that the feather, housed in a display case next to a picture of Ted, was stolen last year, with a stag party from Leeds the main suspects. We sit down by a carved, vertical route map of the Pennine Way next to an open fire, numb and not particularly talkative, more interested in a hot drink than anything alcoholic. A magnet for bikers, hikers and cyclists, the pub has a fancy-dress atmosphere, with most customers togged out in black leather, luminous lycra or multicoloured Gore-tex, all of it damp or partly dried, carrying with it the vague whiff of wet dogs, augmented by the actual presence of a number of wet dogs. After half an hour it's time to move on, but I can't quite pull myself away from the action in the next room, where performance poet Ranting Ritchie has set up his mic stand and is trying to get the attention of customers who are talking and drinking or skewering Cumberland sausages with forks or sawing through the grilled rinds of gammon steaks. He recites a couple of John Cooper Clarke pieces with the swearing edited out, presumably because there are kids and families present, and he has a good line in banter, but it's hard going. I feel a strong surge of schadenfreude, watching him trying to work the crowd and rise above the clinking of glasses and the chatter of pub-goers, seeing it from the other side. It's a reaction not unlike vertigo, a horrible sense that at any moment I might reach for the microphone and jump with him into the poetic abyss, in a poetic suicide pact, and I'm swaying and sweating by the door when Peter's hand lands on my shoulder and steers me out onto the moor.

*

From Tan Hill to Keld is all downhill, or at least it seems that way compared with what came before, and the miles go past quickly and without incident, the wind dropping, the weather cheering up, the temperature rising. But fourteen miles is still a fair step in one day. I'm feeling it in my calves, and Peter has pulled something in his leg, and is now less concerned with how far to the nearest tenth of a mile we have walked and more preoccupied with how far we have to go. Paul seems to be going well but is quieter, as we all are. Then rounding the shoulder of Low Brown Hill my mood brightens. The valley ahead runs directly south, and as we enter it, the clouds dissolve and sunlight fills it from top to bottom, a big bath of buttery yellow light spread right to our feet. Not only that, it's a 'dale', not the first dale I've walked into or across but the first one that actually *looks* like a dale, Stonesdale actually, a typical, picture-book, pop-up dale, with lime-green grass partitioned into fields by white dry-stone walls, fringed by moor, a small brook running through it, tidy windowless barns at the end of cart-tracks, a single farmhouse with a single tree giving it shelter, a yard to the side and a kitchen garden to the rear, and doves on the roof. And then it hits me that I'm cheerful not only in response to the postcard prettiness opening up ahead but out of a realisation that I have walked into Yorkshire. Down by the waterfall, before Keld village, a male redstart waits on the branch of a rowan tree just long enough for me to see the fire in its belly and the afterburn of its tail.

*

I'm reading at the Georgian Theatre Royal in Richmond, a place that has to be seen to be believed, or perhaps believed to be seen. Built in 1788 by actor–manager Samuel Butler, closed down sixty years later and remaining closed until the year I was born, the theatre is a kind of optical illusion, somehow seating up to two hundred people in an auditorium reminiscent of an old operating theatre, like the one Keats attended in London, or an early provincial courtroom, just as likely to host a murder trial as a play or poetry reading. Walking onto the stage I feel about a hundred foot tall, looming over the audience, their heads dotted around its galleries and side-boxes like fruit in a market. My feet seem particularly enormous, great clodhopping shoes stretching out in front of me down the raked stage, as if I might squash half the people sitting in the pit by taking a step forward. Attendance is a contested fifty-nine (I've been taking photographs of the audience every night and I can count at least sixty-eight faces in the image) who part with a very generous £270, which I split with the theatre. The audience also parts with one pair of woollen walking socks, one packet of walking plasters and one packet of Garibaldi biscuits, which I keep for myself. It's the first formal reading I've given since Abbotsford, and during the interval I draw the raffle. First prize, a book of poems by Simon Armitage; second prize, two books of poems, etc., etc.

I'm staying with Ben and Delphine who live just up the hill. The routine is familiar by now but the situation still strange: showering in someone else's bathroom, drying off with their towels, shaving amongst their personal toiletries and preferred products, eating at their table, doing my best to be poetic in their company, cashing up on the bedspread, making notes until the small hours, hunting for the light switch. Stranger still for my hosts, I imagine, having a complete outsider disappear behind the door of the spare bedroom, rooms which are nearly always reliquaries or shrines, museums of past lives or mausoleums devoted to a particular absence, a place of mothballed clothes, stockpiled books, musical instruments locked in cases, photographs under cellophane, framed certificates, dusty trophies, threadbare soft toys, objects which have no function or place in the everyday world of the living room or the kitchen or the master bedroom but whose significance to family lore borders on the sacred. I am sleeping in a memory vault, and none of the memories are mine. From the crammed bookshelf I prise out a Penguin paperback copy of the *Odyssey*, well thumbed and riddled with marginalia written in an alien hand, and drift off to sleep with Odysseus still several years from home.

Keld to Hawes

12.5 MILES
OS Explorer OL30 North Sheet/South

Monday 19 July

I wake early and take stock. Was that inked vertical stripe in the subway under the A66 really the halfway line? If so, I'm on the back nine, the home stretch; I have 'broken its back' without it breaking me. Conversely, it means I have the same distance to walk as I have already walked (and I feel like I have walked about five thousand miles) but with only eight days left to do it, and that is a depressing thought. Another week of walking and talking, the plod, plod, plod of my own footsteps and the blah, blah, blah of my own voice. It's raining outside, and if it's raining in Richmond it's almost certainly raining even harder at the top of Swaledale, which means it's probably lashing down in the hills beyond. From the window of the back bedroom I look towards those hills but they have been absorbed by fog. I think about trying to get the weather forecast on my mobile phone but weather forecasts are designed for people wondering whether they should take an umbrella with them to Tesco's, not for people spending their days above the tree-line and inside the clouds. It's a horizontal-based service, and my requirements these days are always vertical.

Although at least I'm not alone, having been assigned Colin Chick, Pennine Way Ranger for the Yorkshire Dales National Park for today's stretch of the journey. Colin looks a tad apprehensive when I stroll towards his regulation green Land Rover and tap on the window, but mellows after just a few minutes of chat, and later on admits to being somewhat uneasy about the prospect of spending eight hours on the hills with a poet.

'What did you think I'd be like?'

'I don't know, to be honest.'

'Some kind of bespectacled, fragile intellectual in a velvet jacket and unsuitable shoes, right?'

'No,' he says, unconvincingly, then a moment later, 'OK, yes.'

I tell him my frilly blouse and pantaloons got dirty on Sleightholme Moor and are at the cleaners, then we set off back towards the waterfall where I spotted the redstart. We're heading for the pretty market town of Hawes in Wensleydale, all cake shops and antiques by reputation,

sitting directly south of here with the massive, arching rump of Great Shunner Fell accounting for everything in between. But first the route insists on a 270-degree clockwise circumnavigation of Kisdon, a sort of five-hundred-metre conical roundabout at the junction of the River Swale and Straw Beck, generating enough centrifugal energy to propel the hiker towards Great Shunner Fell's summit then over the top into the next dale. The path is stony and slippery to begin with, and the hillside rabbit-infested. There's even a small, sable-black bunny, offspring of some escaped pet, presumably, that hasn't quite evolved to meet the requirements of the wild, and crouches about five yards away with its head in a wall, on the basis that if he can't see us then we can't see him. A couple of buzzards glide over the ravine to our left. This was an old corpse road, though it's tricky enough to negotiate with just the weight of a medium-size rucksack strapped across the back, and I really wouldn't fancy trying to bear a dead body along these broken and slimy rocks. The path to heaven does not run smooth, and this particular path is less smooth than most. In keeping with his Land Rover, Colin is wearing a green fleece top, a green shirt, green socks and a pair of green shorts, and the view, as I follow him up and around the clock-face of Kisdon, is mainly his sturdy calves and the odd flash of thigh. The buzzards are still circling, and a kestrel hangs in the valley, its wings wavering and balancing in the breeze but its head so still it could be nailed in position. Colin says there are white crows to look out for in Malhamdale but none here. Splashing through a patch of heather, he stoops to pick a handful of bilberries, shining like tiny purple baubles, luminous globes overhanging the path, so bright because dazzling sunlight is suddenly reflecting from the rain-coated skin of the fruit, and I notice an unusual presence walking along beside me for a few minutes, someone I haven't seen for a while: my shadow.

The door to Kisdon Cottage is locked so we peer through the window. We've stopped here because Colin says it is the house of his dreams. It's empty but not abandoned: the flagged floor looks swept, there's a red-and-white gingham cloth on the kitchen table, candlesticks are streaked with molten wax, and crockery and ornaments are arranged tidily on the dresser shelves and across the mantelpiece. Outside there's a plastic washing line strung between the gable end and the porch, and even the semblance of a kitchen garden bordered by a low stone wall. I can't tell if Colin is disappointed by these signs of life or pleased that the property is habitable.

'Can you get a car up here?'

'Near enough,' he says, but he isn't looking at me or the house, and I realise as I follow his gaze that for Colin, Kisdon Cottage is less about cosy firesides and wooden staircases taken back to the grain, and more about the view. Because the whole of Swaledale is rolled out in front of us, eastward-facing and filled with early sun, home to a long, lazy river, a textbook dale straight out of a Sunday-night ITV drama or an advert for something wholesome and organic. On the OS map, which I lift and hold along our line of sight, Swaledale lies stretched, pale and thin, like the sloughed, diaphanous skin of an anaconda, or the pelt of a long-by-narrow creature staked out on the ground. The white background accorded to it, against the pale yellow of the moors, even makes it appear like a parched salt pan or an estuary at low tide. Whereas in reality the reverse is true, the fields and meadows being lush with colours and rich in textures, and the moors above it becoming faint and ill-defined to the point where they merge and blur with the sky. From this vantage point, Kisdon Cottage feels like and may literally be the highest house in Swaledale, standing above it all at the valley head, having the finest outlook, the final say.

Thwaite, when we clomp through, seems all rental cottages and tea shops, and the noise of our boots as we walk stride for stride up the narrow main street sounds intrusive and exaggeratedly yobbish, enough to bring every hanging basket and quaint chimney pot crashing to the earth. At a stile just outside the village, Colin proudly points out one of the solid oak Pennine Way signs which he himself commissioned. To prove its robustness he thumps it with the heel of his hand, and it trembles momentarily before resuming its solidity and stillness, its strong arm pointing unwaveringly west. Half a mile later he bends down and without breaking stride scoops up a yellow flower growing at the side of a wall.

'Tormentil, good for headaches and hangovers,' he says, before nipping the stalk between his thumb and forefinger and biting off the head.

'Well?' I ask him as he stands there ruminating.

'Well,' he says, and we begin the toiling, heavy ascent of the Fell, leaning into the gradient, putting our shoulders to gravity's wheel. In shape, Great Shunner resembles a splayed horseshoe, and our ascent follows the south-east-facing rim, with Buttertubs Pass to the left under a distant cairn called Lovely Seat. It's slow going but we're lured and enticed across one section by a distressed and animated golden plover. I don't recall ever seeing one of these birds close up, or bearing witness to its 'goldenness' in such definition and resolution without the aid of binoculars. Trying to draw us away from a nest or its young, this female keeps flapping into the air then coming down about twenty yards or so in front, peep-peeping conspicuously, wanting us to follow or chase, and because it keeps landing on the path we're happy to do just that, a win–win situation, the bird believing its diversion strategy has worked, me and Colin glad of the company and the encouragement. It takes us to an area which, if it were on a golf course, would be cordoned off with 'Ground Under Repair' notices, thirty or forty square yards either side of the path which Colin has sown with Natural England Upland Grass Seed Mix to combat the effects of erosion, and the seeds seem to have sprouted. He shoos a few sheep away from his unlikely and implausible garden, and when I say to him that growing grass up here must be like painting the Forth Rail Bridge, he just shrugs, tears open a Mars Bar and strides on.

'This stone needs re-laying,' he says a little further along a length of causey paving, or, 'I'll have to come back and mend that,' where two or three planks of duckboard have rotted away. It's impressive that someone should take such a detailed interest in this remote place, noting the slightest defect or evidence of disrepair, and nothing short of amazing that he can talk about little patches of ground and small sections of the path as if they were a uniquely different *terroir* from the last or the next, in a landscape which to my eye consists of nothing but undifferentiated wilderness. On the grassy bank above a peat ditch he waits for me while I stuff my coat into the rucksack and refold the map, lying on his back, bare knees in the air, like one of those adult-kids in *Blue Remembered Hills*, agreeing with me that there are worse jobs in the world, belly-laughing through a mouthful of chocolate. In fact every time Colin turns around he seems to have something in his mouth, be it a wild flower, a turkey sandwich, a handful of wine gums or a stalk of grass. 'Can't beat a bit of sugar,' he says ripping into a packet of Starburst, and I have to admire a man who finds time in his life for both chemically derived chewy fruit sweets *and* naturally occurring herbal remedies. He strides ahead again, the stone flags burping and squelching under his big boots, until we begin the final scramble to the top. On this steep ascent, Colin's handiwork includes a long stair-carpet of coir matting to hold a crumbling peat bank in place, and several new steps, built around or to the side of some original steps which look medieval, or at the very least a couple of hundred years old.

'Are they ancient?' I ask him.

'Yep.'

'When do they date back to?'

'Nineteen-eighties.'

*

We eat on the summit, in the cross-shaped, stone-built shelter with wooden beams to sit on, and take the north-facing seat, out of the wind. I feel as if we've really accelerated to the top at a brisk pace, but time and distance are hard to gauge in these climes, and a couple who we passed just outside Thwaite, slower and heavier units than ourselves, are only ten minutes behind us, and crack open a tin of biscuits in the next booth. I can't see them, behind the wall, but I can smell their coffee, and can hear their giggling and the sound of chubby fingers prising bourbons and custard creams out of the plastic packaging. Someone else appears from nowhere, a woman walking a dog, then a couple of hikers, and suddenly all four bays are taken, although no words are exchanged, and we all get on with our lunches and snacks and mobile-phone conversations in the privacy of our own right angles.

Colin points out certain hills to the west and north, the panorama becoming more apparent as the cloud cover begins to fragment and sunlight brings distant peaks into sharper focus. Broad moorland ranges extend one way, punctuated by distinct and isolated prominences, with the more dramatic, clustered and unmistakable presence of the Lake District forming a serrated horizon to the west. He says, 'Cross Fell looks clear. Be lovely up there today.'

The path leading south from the summit is an obvious lane of bright green grass, like a strip of turf flanked by rougher and darker vegetation, and beyond the plateau the way ahead is straightforward to the eye – a steady descent down the spine of a wide but tapering spur pointing directly into Wensleydale. You could close your eyes, curl in a ball and roll from here, and you'd probably end up in the right place. Colin powers on, his giant boots driving straight through puddles and bogs like some robust, heavy-duty military vehicle, with me dancing around in his wake, trying to island-hop between clumps of grass and slippery stones down a track which seems to double as a stream. As on the way up, he points out little areas of his own handiwork or makes a mental note of future repairs and projects he might undertake. We're looking at a stand of dark green trees above Cotterdale, home to a colony of red squirrels, apparently, when a comedy troupe of a dozen rooks comes bowling and barging along the valley side, flapping and cronking, a kind of pantomime funeral party being tumbled and flustered by the wind, then being utterly upstaged and outnumbered by a squadron of twenty or so golden plover flying in formation and at dizzying speed overhead, turning together in an instant then sweeping south until they become little more than a glitter of gold-dust in the far distance before disappearing into the sun.

Eventually we stumble off the track, via Bluebell Hill, and onto the bridge by the Green Dragon pub, which owns or at least acts as the tollgate for Hardraw Force. Hardraw is England's highest waterfall, highest only in the sense that it is the *highest above ground*, apparently, a distinction I can't really begin to understand, though not something which unduly troubled Wordsworth when he visited here. Writing to Coleridge in 1799, he reported that, 'After cautiously sounding our way over stones of all colours and sizes, encased in the clearest water formed by the spray of the fall we found the rock, which had before appeared like a wall, extending itself over our heads like the ceiling of a huge cave, from the summit of which the water shot directly over our heads into a basin, and among the fragments wrinkled over with masses of ice as white as snow, or rather, as Dorothy said, like congealed froth. The water fell at least ten yards from us and we stood directly behind it.' So with Wordsworth having left his literary stamp on the place, and having already splurged on waterfall superlatives at High Force a couple of days ago, I decide to give it a miss, and head straight towards Hawes village along an old, slabbed path which follows the top edge of a sheep pasture, which was once a golf course. After crossing Haylands Bridge, where two young boys are attempting a high-wire act on the wall above the river, I say goodbye and thank you to Colin, who marches off towards a building under the trees with muddy Land Rovers parked outside, which he refers to as his office, though I can't imagine Colin ever being content to push a pen or prod a keyboard for more than a few minutes every day, and surely his real office is not a room in a building at all but the great outdoors, or at least that part of it occupied by Great Shunner Fell. I wish him luck. I wish him Kisdon Cottage.

Hawes's reputation for old furniture emporiums and pastry outlets seems entirely justified looking through the shop windows on the main street; I don't need a Victorian nest of tables or a Belfast sink right now but I can't resist a pork pie, even though I'm within half a mile of a meal, and I'm still wiping the crumbs from my mouth when I knock at a big house like a rectory or vicarage in what might be a suburb or satellite of Hawes, if a market town of twelve hundred people is allowed such a thing, and watch for signs of movement through the stained glass in the door. I've never met Ann Pilling but I've read her poems, and I've seen the books *Henry's Leg* and *Amber's Secret* on my daughter's bookshelf. She says, 'You're early,' having opened the door, looked me up and down and figured out that the stubbly, wind-burnt, pastry-speckled face must belong to Simon Armitage, her guest for tonight. 'And filthy,' I tell her. Following her instructions I park my boots in the porch and strip off as many peat-coated, sweat-stained layers as is decently possible, then follow her through to the back of the house where several women are grouped around a teapot or toasting their backsides on the cooking range. I think I know them all, or some of them, but I'm too befuddled by walking to recall where or when I've met them before, or to remember their names, or understand why they should all be gathered in Ann Pilling's kitchen. I gobble down a sizeable lump of sponge cake before a tour of the house leads me to my bedroom, a large high-ceilinged room with big furniture and a vast fireplace to one side with the words 'Lord Keep My Memory Green' carved in the stone above it. After a bath I fall asleep in a four-poster bed, the canopy overhead keeping the rain out of my dreams. Then wake about an hour later, listening to Ann's husband, Joe, issuing parking guidelines outside in the yard, and hearing the growing chatter of voices downstairs. I lie on the bed for a while longer, watching five starlings perched on a set of telephone wires outside the window, like notes on a page of sheet music, and try to hum the tune, until another car arrives and pomps its horn, and the starlings scatter. Then I brush my teeth, tug a comb through my hair, glue on a smile and gather up my poems.

I have to admire Ann for throwing open the doors of her house to the general public. I wouldn't. Chairs have been arranged in rows in the drawing room, right to the very front, so I have to scootch back against the mantelpiece to find room to stand and read without treading on someone's toes or sitting in their lap. Not that I leap about or anything, or even move, or even take my eyes off the page. It is, from a visual perspective, little more than a man in a creased shirt holding a book in his hand for three quarters of an hour. But in terms of my requirements it's completely quiet, there being no shortage of silence in this part of the world, and intimate, and friendly, and I'm touched that fifty people should venture out to a private house in a distant corner of North Yorkshire on a damp Monday night to hear poetry, some from as far away as Burnley and Leeds. In what feels to be a trusting and confessional atmosphere, and thinking again of journeys, both psychological as well as literal, I read a poem called 'Roadshow', set in Cornwall at the time of the 1999 eclipse, when St Ives was like Bethlehem at census time, with neither a meal nor bed to be had for love nor money. On hearing there was a Radio 1 roadshow being held on the rugby field at the top of the town, and still clinging to the idea that we were young and in touch, we decided to walk there, even though my wife was heavily pregnant and the lanes were narrow and steep. It took a good hour to climb the hill, hearing the drums and guitar chords and seeing the pulsing lights on the horizon, stopping every hundred yards or so to sit down and draw breath. But the very instant we crossed the touchline the show came to an abrupt end, and suddenly there were several hundred youthful, beautiful and energetic people swarming past us in the other direction, hungry for action and life. It was the end of one thing and the beginning of another, a complete coincidence and the perfect metaphor. It was a poem.

It's not until I finish reading that I notice out of the corner of my eye the overspill crowd, half a dozen of them sitting on an assortment of chairs and stools in the hallway, and another four or five peering through the banister rails, like children who've crept downstairs after bedtime to spy on the grown-ups. They might be clutching teddy bears or sucking their thumbs. Or yawning. Or asleep.

Hawes to Horton-in-Ribblesdale

14 MILES

OS Explorer OL30 South Sheet, OL2 West

Tuesday 20 July

After handing over a stretched and bulging sock containing a staggering £247, Ann and her women wave me off and I set out along the road, creep through the field where the vet was trampled to death by cattle last year, hop over a gate and follow Gaudy Lane past Gaudy House Farm towards the edge of the moor. Which is not gaudy at all, either in shape or form, but blotted out by heavy mist, and even though I'm happy, excited even to be walking alone and to have the day to myself, all that elation evaporates as soon as I climb above four hundred feet, where I am absorbed by clouds. I lose the path very quickly, but I'm too miserable to worry about it, and eventually stumble across a few old footprints in the mud, then a line of worn grass through a bit of a heath, then a stile and eventually a sign, and without trying or particularly caring I'm back on track. Days in Cloudland can be a test of nerve and intelligence, especially on high ground or across remote and dangerous terrain, but on sections like today, a relatively straightforward traverse between two dales with towns anchoring each end of the line and none-too-distant roads on either side, they're a test of imagination. Because without a view, the whole enterprise is pointless, a futile schlep, hours of visual confinement with nothing to see apart from your own feet, and nothing to do apart from carry on. The mist also exhibits properties of false hope, most notably a mirage effect, where sunlight seems always on the point of breaking through and where brightness and clarity seem always within reach, just beyond the next veil of fog, just a few steps ahead, the feeling that at any moment, particularly while ascending, you might *emerge*, like a rocket escaping the earth's atmosphere, and be rewarded with a 360-degree view of a billion cubic miles, and stand eyeball to eyeball with the sun. It's a cruel trick. One of the guide books talked about the mysterious and beguiling Snaizeholme Valley, which according to the map must be down to my right as I trudge up the muddy ditch of West Cam Road, but the only mystery is whether or not it exists at all, being nothing but grey mizzle. At times I'm navigating more by a sense of sound than anything else, my ears following the wind as it traces the surrounding topography, implying a hill to the south or a sudden falling away of the land to the north, then bringing the roar of a waterfall, or running water, then the call of an invisible kestrel, and the sound of restless trees, full of rumours and whispered oaths, hundreds of them, close by but hidden from sight.

From nowhere a young man in blue waterproofs appears then disappears after granting me only a millisecond of eye contact and without saying a word. As well as being surprised how few people there are on the Pennine Way, I find it extraordinary how many of them don't want to chat or even exchange a few pleasantries, and simply power past with their heads down and their hands in their pockets. In fact I've been keeping a record of hikers heading in the opposite direction, making prejudicial assumptions about their motivation based entirely on physical appearance and general demeanour. Here's the tally so far:

Where I fit into this taxonomy of walking types I wouldn't like to say, just as I can't find the right category for the father-and-son team who come plodding up Cam High Road just after Kidhow Gate, although they are certainly my favourites so far. In the cloud I don't see them till they're a few yards away, the boy wiry and blond, about ten or eleven, in combat trousers and with a penknife clipped to his belt, his father overweight and scarlet-faced, stripped down to his vest, out of breath under a heavy pack. But there's an aura around them which is more than just steam or mist, the boy looking adoringly up at his dad, the dad staring proudly ahead, the son proving to the father that he isn't too young and the father proving to the son that he isn't too old. And I like them even more when they stop for a chat, the dad reeling off their itinerary so far, the boy echoing his every word, verifying every fact and figure, every spot-height and distance, regurgitating his encyclopaedic knowledge of the Pennine Way after swallowing it whole.

'Plain sailing down to Old Ing,' says the father. 'About five miles.'

'Five and a quarter,' the son chips in.

I tell them that the mist is bad all the way to Hawes, but the father says it won't be a problem if they stick to the guide book.

'Which one are you using?'

'The bible,' he says.

'Wainwright,' says the son.

The father lifts his hand to show me the *Pennine Way Companion*, with one of Alfred Wainwright's trademark sketches on the blue-and-white cover, below his trademark signature. 'Can't fault it,' he says, holding it out towards me, the bookmark of his squat red thumb inserted between dog-eared, rain-blotted pages. The son then raises his own identical copy of the book, open at the same place, and when the wind riffles the paper I notice boyish handwriting in the columns and rows of the back pages, numbers and words in blue and red ink, his own personal record of departure times and arrival times and weather conditions, diligently entered in the 'Reader's Log' which Wainwright thought-fully provided for the more statistically inclined walker. We go our separate ways, but when I glance backwards I notice that the boy has slipped his arm through the hook of his father's elbow. Then they disappear into the mist. A few minutes later I pass about seven or eight elderly ramblers sitting on a grass bank eating sandwiches, saturated with drizzle, staring into the fog and singing, 'Oh I do like to be beside the seaside, oh I do like to be beside the sea.'

As far as I can tell Alfred Wainwright was a funny old stick. My memory of him is entirely derived from television documentaries which may have become muddled with *Fast Show* sketches and episodes of *The League of Gentlemen*, so he always comes to mind as a somewhat curmudgeonly character, extolling the beauty of one hill while damning the ugliness of another, a man with silver glasses, silver hair under a flat cap and a pipe between his teeth, often picking his way very slowly across some scree slope or boulder-heap in decidedly pre-modern walking apparel, before rendezvousing with a woman called Betty in a misted-up Austin 1100 in a quarry in Cumbria. Wainwright walked the Pennine Way in 'bits and pieces' over an eighteen-month period, during two foot-and-mouth outbreaks and in what sounds to have been almost constant rain. At the end of his *Pennine Way Companion*, dated New Year 1968, he hopes that fellow walkers enjoy the journey but advises against looking for him anywhere along the route, because 'I've had enough of it.' 'Characterful' would be one way of describing the book, though less charitable critics might be more inclined towards 'chauvinistic', citing his constant use of the male pronoun, his reference to the 'brotherhood' of hikers, his description of the walk as a good excuse for 'getting away from the wife on some 30–40 occasions' (only compounded by the asterisked apology, 'Sorry, girls!') and his comment that on one day he suffered 'the ultimate ignominy of having to shelter under a woman's brolly'. Yet the books are without doubt works of art, and part of that eccentric English tradition in which the oddball amateur working at the personal, local level comes to be regarded eventually as an unparalleled genius with almost universal appeal. In that sense, Wainwright is the William Blake of walking. His dogged obstinacy even resulted in his *Pennine Way Companion* being formatted back to front, on the basis that the north should always be at the top and the south at the bottom, resulting in his running commentary and accompanying strip-maps beginning on page 171 and ending on page 5. For the traditional walker following the recognised route from Edale's starting pistol to Kirk Yetholm's chequered flag this is probably a bit annoying, but for me, matching Wainwright's contrariness stride for stride, page for page, it is inadvertently convenient. Opposite the iconic handwriting and scrupulous cartography, on the evenly numbered pages, are some three hundred drawings of bridges, stiles, copses, churches, cairns, houses, fences, walls, landmarks and features of every type, which despite being grainy, black-and-white sketches seem to radiate with a sense of precision and texture, and speak of Wainwright the draughtsman, a man determined to make everything as clear and exact as possible but to do so in his own way, or not to do it at all.

*

In my own way I'm making good progress today, despite the fog, or perhaps even because of it, with no view or vista to divert and distract, and that alluring, elusive brightness always just up ahead, tempting me forward at full speed. One becalmed stretch of heath is populated by nothing other than thistles, some purple-headed, others topped with flaring white plumes, a lot of them a good five foot in height, absolutely perpendicular, symmetrical and still, ghostly in the mist, a further discouragement against dawdling or slackening the pace. In fact I am surging on, veritably powering forth, so much so that I've crossed the halfway point of today's section well before lunchtime and an hour later am on the long slow descent into Horton-in-

Ribblesdale, with Ribblesdale itself dutifully opening up to the west and its main settlement emerging in the distance, a cluster of houses under the black border of a railway line and beneath the gaping white cavity of a limestone quarry, as if the hillside had lost a tooth. Distance, I've come to realise, is not the determining factor in terms of travelling time – it's all about terrain. Today's leg is fourteen miles, but much of that is flattened track, mostly downhill, and the wind has followed me all the way. In terms of hours it's probably the equivalent of an eight-mile walk over two high peaks, and about half the effort. Falling towards Horton I can now see that the quarry is terraced or 'benched', and semicircular, like a giant amphitheatre facing the town, and today's performance includes a man on a ride-on mower cutting candy-stripes into the grass on the football field, and a fly-past of several Canada geese. Far from slowing up on approach I seem to be accelerating, speeding down the rutted and water-scored track where rain has dumped the hill's moraine in great piles on every corner and bend, then overshooting the rendezvous point of New Inn by several hundred metres, crossing the river and following the road all the way to the railway station, which is closed, as is Horton itself, it seems, before doubling back and ping-ponging around the empty streets until I run out of momentum and sit down on a wall. Just then a car pulls up, driven by Veronica. I don't know Veronica, but there's a copy of my book *Kid* placed prominently on the dashboard, next to the tax disc, and this being the pre-arranged signal for our assignation I jump in next to her and we drive off into the sunset. Or, as it's sometimes referred to, the Lake District.

*

Grasmere is not on the Pennine Way of course, but giving a reading in the cradle of romanticism has been a date on my calendar every year for well over a decade, originally in the Prince of Wales Hotel but now removed to St Oswald's Church, with Wordsworth's grave just a few yards away, and his presence everywhere. I think of the reading as marking the beginning of summer, even though it usually rains, and often manage a bit of a ramble the next morning before heading back down the M6. One year, just before dawn, I set off up the old Corpse Road behind Dove Cottage, past the Coffin Stone, and after watching big metallic-coloured dragonflies zooming around above the glassy surface of a small duck pond, I headed directly up the hill towards Alcock Tarn. I had a yellow Labrador with me, which I'd unwittingly adopted for a couple of days. About halfway up the hill I stopped for a breather and let the dog off the lead, and away it went, crashing around in the bracken, chasing through the undergrowth doing its doggy things before eventually running out of steam and padding back towards me to sit panting and slavering at my feet. I'd shinned up to the top of a high dry-stone wall, and was looking back down towards the lake, the surface of which was completely unbroken, lying there like spilt mercury under the brightening sky. And that's when I saw the deer. And not just any deer but a red deer, a stag, no more than twenty yards away under the lower branches of a chestnut tree, a big beast, side on, in profile, with a constellation of flies fizzing around its nose and another set at its rear end. I was close enough to see the contoured grain of its antlers,

close enough even to see the dark, upturned limpet of its eye looking at everything in its orbit, everything apart from me, it seemed, because by some miracle I swear it hadn't seen me, or heard me, and hadn't heard the dog either. Neither had the dog got wind of the stag. I'd witnessed its reaction to sheep on several occasions, and knew for a fact it would have been exhilarated beyond control at the prospect of a wild deer. But for a few minutes, then a few minutes more, I just perched there on top of that wall, arbiter and sole observer of these two separate worlds, the world of the dog and the world of the stag, hunter and hunted, between which no sound or sight or scent could pass, apparently. And for as long as the event lasted, I felt as if I straddled two entirely distinct dimensions: how else to explain how these two finely tuned creatures with their hyper-receptive senses and hair-trigger nerves could be so close yet so completely unaware of each other's existence.

Eventually the deer lumbered away up the hill, out of the shadow of the tree and into the morning light, so I could see now the redness of its fur, muted and streaky, like something dyed in blood then washed in water. Just as it crossed the horizon the great candelabra of its antlers became silhouetted against the torch of the sun, still low in the sky, and appeared to catch fire. Then off it went into the woods, igniting each copse and thicket with its flaming horns, spreading the morning as it went.

*

Wordsworth was the poet–walker par excellence. Writing about Wordsworth's legs, his friend Thomas De Quincey once remarked, 'undoubtedly they had been serviceable legs beyond the average standard of human requisition; for I calculate, upon good data, that with these identical legs Wordsworth must have traversed a distance of 175 to 185,000 English miles.' From his sister Dorothy's journals we can build up a comprehensive assessment of William's walking habits, and I'm particularly fond of an entry from Monday 14 December 1801 stating that 'Wm and Mary walked to Ambleside in the morning to buy mousetraps'. By Saturday of the same week, by my rough calculation, he had walked a further twenty-five miles, pottering between errands and engagements in freezing conditions and with snow on the ground. Even in later life, a five-mile round trip to the hardware store or twenty-mile perambulation was hardly a rare occurrence, but these distances should be viewed as a gradual slowing down considering the marathons of his youth, most notably in 1790 when instead of revising for his exams at Cambridge he went walkabout in the French Alps with his friend Robert Jones. They covered some three hundred miles in two weeks; his autobiography in verse, *The Prelude*, not published until after his death and detailing much of the expedition, takes about the same time to read and would probably extend to the same distance if laid end to end. In the best passages, the blank verse by which Wordsworth describes the journey operates both as an indulgence and a restraint, encouraging a flowing, lyrical style suited to the intoxication of travel and the excitement of youth, but always at a measured and regular pace, so in every way it is a poem which goes by foot. To my mind, the best overview of Wordsworth's great tour comes in Richard Holmes's book *Footsteps: Adventures of a*

Romantic Biographer, in which Holmes shadows Wordsworth's experience of revolutionary France, combining literary criticism, personal memoir and a kind of biographical stalking to produce an altogether new form of travel writing. But the most compelling chapter is its opening one, in which the eighteen-year-old Holmes dons a brown felt hat and walks in the footsteps and hoofprints of Robert Louis Stevenson and his troublesome donkey from Le Monastier to St Jean-du-Gard in 1878, a walk of 220 kilometres through the 'French highlands', which Stevenson completed in under a fortnight. For all of Holmes's encounters with farmers, waitresses, peewits and dogs, there's a developing sense that his true companion through the Cévennes is Stevenson himself, often in the form of his twenty-three-thousand-word journal, written en route. 'For my part, I travel not to go anywhere, but to go . . . the great affair is to move; to feel the needs and hitches of life a little more nearly; to get down off this feather bed of civilisation, and to find the globe granite underfoot and strewn with cutting flints.' That's Holmes quoting Stevenson. Holmes treading in Stevenson's footsteps, and a quarter of a century later, me riding on the shirt tail of Holmes.

Horton-in-Ribblesdale to Malham

15 MILES
OS Explorer OL2 West Sheet/South

Wednesday 21 July

I'm not on a literary pilgrimage, and have no presiding poetic spirit to guide me through the Pennines, but as of yesterday evening I do have my own Robert Jones, in the shape of Slug, a friend from college, who came sauntering around the corner of St Oswald's last night with his anorak tied around his middle, a big grin on his face and nowhere to stay. I blag him a ticket for the reading and a three-course dinner (i.e. give him my meal then pay for my own) but when he starts eyeing the settee in my guest-house room as a possible bed for the night I have to draw the line. Slug is a geography graduate. Just. Despite which, he seems blissfully unaware of the popularity of the Lake District during holiday season, and is lucky to eventually find a vacancy at a nearby B&B. And blissfully unaware that the Pennine Way does not pass through Grasmere, so is surprised when we have to cadge a lift back to Horton-in-Ribblesdale to resume the trail.

'Have you got any lunch with you?' I ask him.

'Not really. What sort of sandwiches have you got?'

'Nothing you'd like. If we buy some, have you got a rucksack to put them in?'

'Not really. But I could put them in yours.'

Andy from the Wordsworth Trust drops us in the car park, and I tell him to forget my fee for the reading, not because I'm Mr Moneybags but because it falls outside the terms and conditions of my walk, not to mention beyond its geographical boundaries, and I'm still determined to play by the rules. Then we go looking for a shop.

*

The phrase 'happy-go-lucky' could have been made for Slug. He wears the sunniness of his Cornish ancestry (actual surname Slegg) in his laugh and in his attitude, and always seems to land on his feet, no matter what heights he throws himself from or how many rotations he makes during the descent. So it doesn't surprise me in the least when the only shop open in town is the Horton-in-Ribblesdale Tourist Information Centre incorporating the Pen-y-ghent cafe, stockists of both three-cheese brown-bread sandwiches and walking gear, though he is less fortunate in his choice of rucksack, which we realise later in the day is designed for a small child. The proprietor recognises me and insists on taking a photograph while I sign the visitors' book, then insists on another photograph but this time with my sleeves rolled up, prompting Slug to ask him if he is a forearm fetishist. As well as his cheery disposition, the other thing I like about Slug is that he doesn't get all his ideas from the same place, so while he is on the one hand a tree-hugging, hedge-planting vegetarian topiarist who goes on dry-stone-walling weekends and watches Fred Dibnah DVDs, he is also a wisecracking, weird-minded, nocturnal, hedonistic Leeds United-supporting metrosexual south Londoner when he wants to be.

'Why didn't you tell me you were coming?'

'Thought I'd surprise you.'

'How long are you walking for?'

'All the way. Unless it's too far. Windermere?'

'Where are you staying?'

'Dunno. But don't worry. You'll think of something.'

*

Today's stage is all about two summits, and one of those annoying days when instead of getting on with the job of heading south the Way strikes out in several compass directions, including north, in order to drag the weary traveller over Pen-y-ghent and Fountains Fell, just because *they're there*. Pen-y-ghent (possibly translated as 'hill on the border') is the smallest of that trio of summits often lumped together as the Three Peaks, Ingleborough being the next highest and Whernside the big daddy at just a few flagpoles short of 2,500 feet. To become a member of the Three Peaks Club the twenty-five-mile route connecting the hills must be circumnavigated in less than twenty-four hours. There's also a Three Peaks Fell Race where knotty, knobbly, knuckled, pain-retardant people in numbered bibs somehow get around the course in about three hours, and a cyclo-cross version, where similarly formed and attired people do it even faster but with a bicycle on their shoulders.

True to form the summit is covered in mist as we set off up the walled, bumpy track of Horton Scar Lane, so we don't get to see the classic double profile, where the millstone grit cap of the hill juts out above the limestone plinth it rests on. Instead we see what looks to be an almost vertical path heading directly into the clouds, like a ladder into heaven, and about halfway up it a big yellow digger. I recall Colin saying something about working up here today and fancy that we might be in for a round of wine gums or a quick herbal remedy at the very least, but when we reach it the digger is inactive and forlorn, its metal tracks sinking into the soft ground, its long articulated arm propping it against the slope, the giant claw full of dirt and stones. It seems more abandoned than unattended, and utterly incongruous, like the London bus pulled out of Antarctic ice and the Second World War bomber found on the moon – except this is real. When I try the glass-panelled door it swings open, but there are no keys in the ignition, and I even wonder if this is what passes for joy-riding in these parts, hot-wiring a four-ton excavator and ditching it halfway up one of England's highest peaks. Such thefts usually end in immolation, and the Pennine moors where I live are dotted with the rusting carcasses of burnt-out cars, the make and model unrecognisable in charred, skeletal form, each one an ugly shrine to some act of profitless criminality, the culprits having sloped off to a country bus stop or village railway station for public transport back to wherever they came from. There are no signs of torching here, though in this dampness and in this wind, striking a match to initiate the fire-raising process wouldn't be an easy thing.

In fact the wind is increasing with every contour; at about 1,900 feet when the route swings due south for the diagonal climb to the summit it's a loud and continuous blast, furiously opposed to our progress, one of those streams of air that seems particularly directed at anyone trying to go any further, even if the path is so deeply scored it would be difficult to get out of it, let alone lose it. We presume we're

at the top when we arrive at an S-shaped shelter and hunker down in one of its curves, though the wind doesn't seem to be bothering three Scousers who suddenly pop up from the other side of the hill in T-shirts and shorts and manage to light cigarettes without too much trouble. We chat for a while, their throats full of Liverpudlian fricatives, their mouths full of smoke, which as soon as it leaves their lips is flung backwards at a million miles an hour into the fog-filled north.

The descent from Pen-y-ghent is the closest the Pennine Way comes to rock-climbing, a vertiginous scramble down exposed boulders and loose stones on the hill's most exposed and narrowest aspect, with not much room for manoeuvre and little margin for error. Coming up would be easier, without having to see the land falling away at a disturbing angle or the path disappearing over a precipice, or feeling the hillside crumbling underfoot. In two or three places I even turn around and go down backwards, remembering advice on how to negotiate a stepladder from a friend's loft. A handrail would be good, though frowned on, obviously. Or even a rope – anything for the hands to reach for and the fingers to curl around instead of grabbing at tufts of loosely anchored grass or flapping at thin air. Towards the bottom where the path spills out like broken biscuits we pass about thirty kids and a couple of teachers setting off for the peak, and wonder about the risk-assessment form associated with this kind of day trip, which presumably has to allow for several types of gravity-induced injury all the way from a sprained ankle to death by plummeting.

*

One of the unspoken and perhaps unconscious reasons for choosing geography as a degree, apart from shortcomings in other subject areas at exam level, was the lure of the field trip, the notion of hacking through virgin forest and happening on an undiscovered Amazonian tribe, or tracking the behaviour of a barrage balloon from a weather station somewhere in the Arctic Circle, or driving sand buggies across the Gobi Desert in search of water. The reality of course was far more prosaic: one visit to Welwyn Garden City for a module on new towns, and a tour of the M25. Admittedly things got a little more exotic in the second year, with a trip to the Netherlands then another to Paris. But in Holland, instead of plotting population statistics using records in Nijmegen Public Library, I went in search of other kinds of records, the ones played at thirty-three and a third revolutions per minute, rarities on obscure labels, imports and bootlegs not available in the UK, and instead of grasping the fundamentals of postwar Dutch demographics I came home clutching *Bleke Hender Jeg Har Elsket* by Eyeless in Gaza, and considered it a major requisition. In Paris, the predominantly male geography department had shared the cost of the trip with the entirely female and completely glamorous French studies department, and this time I returned with no understanding whatsoever of Le Corbusier's idealistic proposals for relieving the urban housing crisis (and no vinyl either) but with a passionate interest in Anglo-French relations. It says a great deal about Slug's undergraduate experience, when we start reminiscing, that he can't remember where he went on his field trips, but vaguely recalls standing somewhere near the sea with a soil auger in his hand.

In a field at Rainscar, next to the lane, in a saddle between two valleys, where the gradient decants Silverdale Gill to the south-west and Pen-y-ghent Gill to the north-east, we applaud a young black bullock in a field, so contoured and muscled, so sculpted in every part of its flesh that it looks like a diagram in a butcher's shop displaying all the various cuts of meat. Then we turn ninety degrees and plod towards the top of Fountains Fell, reaching the strange landscape of its summit at lunchtime, old coal workings being responsible for the craters and bunkers that extend across its plateau. Two large cairns, which Wainwright christened the Two Stone Men, stand just to the left of the path, wondrous, defiant and improbable. For two walkers they provide a good backrest, and plenty of shelter, and now that the clouds

are beginning to lift for the first time today, a well-deserved view. And to two geographers that view looks like classic limestone country: wooded river valleys cutting through grazed green slopes, and above them, bold and distinctive hills, shaped and formed rather than angled or peaked, with steel-grey terraces and scars along the shoulder of each ridge, and bone-yards of grey stone on the lower slopes where time and the weather have prised boulders out of their settings and rolled them down the hills. One thing I've learned to expect with the Pennine Way is that even across featureless plains and over wide empty moors, you'll suddenly find yourself in a more localised setting with its own particular atmosphere and boundaries, like the territory we stroll through next, a long easy descent through an area of marsh and bulrush, decorated with wild flowers, strewn stones and docile cows. It could be an idealised scene in a Romantic painting, or even something from the Renaissance, as if a glance over to the right might reveal the Virgin Mary with the infant Christ in her arms, or to the left a satyr carrying a golden spear. The cattle are English longhorns, ruminating and contemplating and not in any way disposed towards confrontation as we pass through the herd, which is a relief, given the armoury available to them. At one point in the mid-seventies there was a craze for replacing the drop-handlebars on a standard racing bike with far wider ones known as cowhorns, which could well have been modelled on this breed. They looked cool but made it difficult to escape down narrow ginnels or snickets after a misdemeanour.

The big glittering mirror set into the landscape in the far distance is Malham Tarn, which is where we're heading, and Adrian saves us the bother of having to track him down by intercepting us just south of Tennant Gill Farm, his frantic sheepdog Maggie rounding us up and bringing us in. Adrian Pickles is the director of Malham Tarn Field Centre, the stately house overlooking the water, and after only a few minutes in his company I begin to get the sense that not only is he one of those experts of the landscape that I've met along the Pennine Way, but in relation to this neck of the woods, its guardian and stock-taker and auditor as well. Barely anything grows here it seems, animal or vegetable, without Adrian's knowledge or even permission, and every millimetre of rain, hour of sunlight or change in wind speed is dutifully measured and entered in the logbooks. A walking encyclopaedia of upper Malhamdale, Adrian is also full of anecdotes and details that put flesh on the bones of the raw data, such as his story about the rare lady's slipper orchid which flowered here last year, so rare that it required round-the-clock protection, which meant someone standing above it during the day and sleeping next to it at night, like the priest at Nemi guarding Diana's sacred grove. Adrian also tells us that during last year's big freeze he ran right across the middle of the tarn, a form of walking on water I suppose.

Not far from his house he leads us through an overgrown meadow, pushes down a clump of nettles with his boot and points to a medium-size puddle, which to Slug and myself, even as two qualified geographers, is a just a medium-size puddle among a clump of nettles, but which is, apparently, the wellspring for an entire river system. Given the eager way Maggie paws and barks at the clear eye of water issuing from the dark hole in the ground it might be the Amazon or the Nile, though for such an excitable creature the dog seems strangely underwhelmed by the presence of a shrew in Adrian's porch, which his wife, Jacqueline, eventually corrals in a Carte D'Or ice-cream tub (Cherry Blossom flavour, I think, or possibly Macadamia Night) and repatriates to the next field while we're drinking tea and eating cake. But there's no time to rest, because I want to walk to Malham, where I bought my first ever pair of walking boots and wrote one of my first ever poems, and want to walk there today rather than add it to tomorrow's journey, even though it means overshooting by a few miles then coming back to the Centre. Plus, Adrian still has a million other things to show us before sundown, many of them rocks.

There's a service road running along the eastern side of the tarn, and the sound of water lapping against a shore is a sound I haven't heard before on this walk. Not a coastal noise of strong wind and big waves and raucous gulls, though no doubt Malham Tarn can boast all those things on its day, but just the composed, rhythmic sound of calm, inland water shushing and slushing against a shallow bank, counterpointing our footsteps on the stony path, and accompanied by the mournful fluting of the odd curlew. The sun is out now, in the south-west, and for a minute or so we walk straight into it, the lake's surface reflecting its glare directly into our faces.

This gentle acreage of upland is the reception area for one of the most remarkable geological features not only along the Pennine Way but in the whole of Britain. Before we go any further though, and because me and Slug have been using the terms loosely and interchangeably, Adrian explains the essential difference between a sink-hole and a swallow-hole, and between a swallow-hole and a shake-hole, and detours us towards a large boulder, a glacial erratic mistakenly known as the Malham meteorite, which is acting like a wobbly plug above some open wound in the ground, around which soil is certainly sinking, or maybe shaking, or perhaps being swallowed. Underneath it I notice a small Tupperware box, and pull it out, thinking someone must have misplaced their picnic. But it turns out that this is a well-known geocache site, a place frequented by geocachers while out geocaching, a practice which has been going on for over a decade now, apparently, without anyone telling me about it. A cross between treasure-hunting and orienteering, geocaching seems to involve navigating to a specific location using a GPS device, finding a waterproof container, signing the logbook with a personalised code name, then making a kind of primitive trading gesture by swapping one trinket or knick-knack for another. Peeling back the lid, it's like looking at the contents of my sock after a particularly eventful reading. Inside there are a few pencils and pens, two gonks, two buttons, an old watch, a golf tee, a badge saying 'Winner' on it, a zebra finger-puppet, and something altogether darker and ritualistic in the form of a lock of hair attached to a poem about cot death. There's also a magpie feather and a polished stone. Adrian says I should make a swap, but the hair and the poem make me feel as if I've intruded, and that taking anything would be tantamount to grave-robbing. Also, the only sentimental things in my wallet are a couple of passport-size photographs, one of my wife and one of my daughter, and I don't feel like leaving either of them in a sandwich box on a lonely moor waiting to be traded for a penny whistle or shark's tooth. So with a little sleight of hand I pretend I've made a transaction, then press the lid onto the container and slide it back under the rock.

No sooner does water pour from the lip of Malham Tarn than it famously disappears again through a hole in the earth. But having talked up this phenomenon as the geographical highlight of the day, the physical reality is something of an anticlimax, water draining away through an ill-defined area of boggy grass either side of a dry-stone wall rather than plunging into a bottomless pit above which vultures circle and rainbows form, although the presence of a couple of hundred glittering silver perch, all lying dead in a small pool, certainly adds a touch of mystery to the scene. Adrian puzzles over the deceased fish, bewildered as to the cause, and a little annoyed, as if this is something which has happened behind his back, some glitch in the local environmental system which will have to be looked into and addressed. I offer my own investigative insight by saying that all the fish appear very healthy-looking.

'Yes. Except for being dead,' he replies.

At the end of the last ice age, melt-water streamed in torrential quantities over the exposed plain of limestone below the tarn, scoring the deep channel that is now the south-running valley known as Watlowes. But limestone is soft, not much more resilient than candy by comparison to certain other rocks, and the constant chemical and abrasive attention of rainwater opened up new channels and short cuts below the surface. Adrian is in his geological element now as we wander along the eerie corridor of the dry valley, which is essentially a dead river. He explains how dyes have been poured in at the top to try to trace the course of the stream as it burrows and tunnels through the complex system of caves and potholes underground, and apparently the water which sinks into the ground at the expertly named Water Sinks is not the same water which eventually emerges as Malham Beck, a mile or so downstream. And we do what we can to preserve our reputation as geographers by going toe-to-toe with him on the terminology, throwing in clints and grikes, then freeze–thaw action, and Slug finally playing an ace by referencing the classic 'karst' scenery associated with the limestone landscape. But no technical explanation can adequately describe what lies ahead. The empty gorge, flanked by sentinels of white stone, littered with rubble and bisected with precarious walls, eventually relaxes its narrow embrace and opens its arms to the astonishing limestone pavement of Malham Cove, ushering

the traveller onto a wide, white platform with a wider panorama beyond. I've only ever approached the Cove from below, from where it looks like a convex dam wall or eighty-metre fortification, a great slab of concrete-coloured rock, forbidding and closed, the end of something, a stop. But from up here it is a beginning. Underfoot, the fractured rocks seem to have been assembled, like large pieces of a three-dimensional jigsaw puzzle, and have a distinct dental look about them – molars and lateral incisors with all the associated cavities and cracks. Tufts of grass sprout from the fissures, even the odd rowan tree, so it's a hop, step and a jump to the front, minding the gaps, being careful not to lose a leg down one of the faults. Standing above the precipice, in the spotlight of late afternoon sun, there's an undeniable sensation of being on stage, with the whole of the world as an audience, or North Yorkshire at the very least. Scanning the horizon I can see a mast to the south-east, which I'm shocked to realise is the television transmitter of Emley Moor, which is only a few miles from my house, and for several moments I pretend to myself that my heart is racing, looping the loop and making some irregular and quite alarming beats. But it's just the mobile phone in my breast pocket, the drone of messages and missed calls that had been circulating the planet all day suddenly spotting me here on top of this cliff and coming swarming into the handset, making it shudder and twitch.

*

Having charmed his way into an evening meal, including an individually cooked vegetarian alternative and a bottle of real ale to wash it down with, Slug is now on the point of being offered a bed for the night. Judging by the way the question of sleeping arrangements is tentatively broached I sense there has been a little bit of behind-the-scenes discussion as to the exact nature of our relationship, not helped by Slug's mischievous references to his many friends in Brighton and his appearance at the dinner table in a pink floral shirt, and eventually I intervene by saying that single rooms would be much appreciated and that I get first use of any shared bathroom and toilet facility. The reading is to take place in the Field Centre itself, leased from the National Trust and converted into an eighty-five-bed residential research facility used mainly by school parties on educational trips to the countryside. Immediately inside the grand entrance there's an office, buzzing with computers and stuffed with handbooks, followed by a couple of high-ceilinged reception rooms and parlours which have been converted into seminar and dining facilities, backed by a couple of kitchens designed for mass catering, and several store rooms stocked with bulk foodstuffs and industrial quantities of ketchup. A Cluedo-like central staircase sweeps upwards to a maze of interconnected dormitories, with ship-style bunk beds built into every recess and heavy fire doors protecting every room. Places like this can never quite shake off the atmosphere of the institution, be it hospital, school, prison or sanatorium, but the many posters and exhibits do their best to conjure up a friendlier ambience, as does the illuminated fish tank crawling with native and under-threat blue crayfish, one of Adrian's pet causes. There's more accommodation across the courtyard, where Slug and myself have been stabled, and another outbuilding converted into classrooms, one of which is tonight's venue.

I don't know where the audience comes from because Malham is a long way from most places and Malham Tarn is a long way from Malham, but they duly arrive, and their numbers are swelled by what I assume to be the enforced attendance of a group of geography students from a school in Norfolk and their two teachers. This week's residents at the Centre, they were probably looking forward to an evening of cigarettes and cider behind the log-shed after a hard day classifying lichen or dissecting owl pellets, but have now been marched along to a poetry reading. 'You don't have to stay,' I tell them, and wait for a minute or so, in silence, with my arms folded, until half a dozen of them pick up their bags and leave.

I read in front of a backcloth of wallcharts and posters showing frogs in their various developmental stages and wild flowers of the British countryside, and to a soundtrack of birdsong and the occasional aeroplane on its way to or from Leeds–Bradford airport. Every now and again I look up at one of the geography teachers, wondering if that could have been me, wondering if, in some other version of reality, it IS me, and that in a moment I'll come to my senses and find myself listening to a poet while trying to plan a lesson on fluvial geomorphology in my head. At the end of the evening the forty-seven people in front of me donate a grand total of £86.96. The sock also contains two corn plasters and an illustrated leaflet describing how to put an injured person in the recovery position: 'Move the patient's nearest arm as though they are stopping traffic.' I assume this contribution has come from a bored student who wanted to let me know how it feels to be the victim of a poetry-trauma, but I find out later that it came from Slug. I also find out that the students were actually looking forward to hearing me read, because they'd been studying my poems for their exams, and only left because I seemed annoyed. I slope off into the kitchen looking for a knife to cut out my tongue, or a slice of humble pie. Other items on the menu are my own foot, which I find I can put in my mouth quite easily, and a bite from the hand that feeds me.

*

I feel I am at the end of my tether
and don't want to go on any longer.
Not like those climbers on Malham Cove –
dipping backwards for their bags of powder,
reaching upwards for the next hairline fracture,
hauling themselves from my binoculars.

And without enlargement they take on the scale
of last night's stars in Malham Tarn,
inching upstream as the universe tilted, mirrored
till we burst their colours with a fistful of cinders.

I follow a line
from the base to the summit, waiting
for something to give, to lose its footing,
for signs of life on other planets.

Malham to Ickornshaw

16 MILES

OS Explorer OL2 South Sheet, OL21 North

Thursday 22 July

Today is a saunter, but a very long one, and tomorrow is the same distance again. I break this news to Slug via the old footballing cliché that 'there will be some tired legs out there', but with his toy rucksack full of finagled sandwiches and 'borrowed' drinks he seems up for it. We're also joined by Carey, a curly-haired reporter from a walking magazine who is writing an article about my trip, who looks like a young Jim Morrison and has brought with him a vintage box camera that doesn't work. I smile for the failed photograph, trying to imagine myself next to an advert for a trekking holiday in Costa Rica and the latest Bill Oddie-endorsed waterproof gaiters. Walking magazines have become a lot sexier over the last decade, Carey says, but also admits that the average age of readership is still the other side of sixty. Retired people, essentially, with time on their hands and the purchasing power sometimes referred to as the grey pound.

'Will I be your cover girl?'

'Centrefold.'

The walk south to Gargrave is a waterside stroll. After being fed by various sikes and streams, Malham Beck swells into the River Aire, and the path on its east bank winds through flowery meadows and past the classic Dales scenery of humpback bridges, cute cottages, trellises hung with sweet peas, stone-built barns, limestone walls, ancient iron gates and fields full of alpacas. Somewhere between Kirkby Malham and Airton a dozen men in cricket jumpers and white tracksuit bottoms come towards us from a bend in the river. They look like the stereotypical village cricket team: the tall one, the short one, the skinny fast bowler and the overweight wicketkeeper, the bank-manager captain who'll open the batting, the tattooed big hitter with the grass-stained trousers, the old spinner and the young lad who'll play if they're a man short. Why a village cricket team should be walking along a Yorkshire riverbank at ten o'clock on a Thursday morning is not clear, and is never explained, but they say hello and we say hello back, and they walk on, a full complement and a twelfth man in search of opposition, ghosts maybe, some legendary local side lost in a storm but who still wander this floodplain once every blue moon, looking for a game. A bit further on there's a show-jumping arena, and for Carey's benefit I jog around it, hurdling the fences in a clockwise direction, except for a refusal at the fifth, a high five-bar gate with a steep ramp on the other side. As I cross the finishing line he clicks away with his malfunctioning Leica.

Carey bows out at Gargrave. We walk on, past several shops which carry my picture in the window, like a wanted man. There's another one on the door of a repair garage, and another on a bus shelter. In three gardens along the main street I've been made into a placard and planted among geraniums, like a Tory councillor looking for re-election, and the several posters tied to the railings of the village hall give me the look of a returning war hero. I keep my head down till we get beyond the last house, but I've been spotted in the main street, and Professor Glyn Turton catches up with us just before we reach the railway line and pass beyond his jurisdiction. Glyn has organised tonight's event and is 'a bit worried about numbers', which in organisational jargon usually implies that apart from himself and possibly two or three reluctant members of his immediate family, there will be no one there. But his explanatory comment, 'With Fire Regulations and so on,' gives me cause for hope. He has also heard that I have a 'travelling companion' with me who doesn't eat meat. I nod my head and point to Slug, who is in the far corner of a field blowing seeds from a dandelion clock, and I apologise for any inconvenience. Glyn assures me that it isn't a problem, and tells me that even as we speak his wife is scouring the shops of Gargrave for edible vegetables. Then having seen us across the parish boundary, he heads back into town.

On we go. More fields. Innumerable gates to open then close again. No consistent path so a lot of map-reading and guesswork. No real views, landmarks or features, but undeniably pleasant, easy on the eye and the feet, a clear day. On we go, agreeing, disagreeing, bragging, bullshitting, confessing, remembering, playing A–Z goalkeepers to kill the time, Almunia, Barthez, Corrigan, having lunch on a canal near a double-arched bridge, Dudek, nothing for E, Félix, striding through Thornton-in-Craven or Craven-in-Thornton, lagging behind, taking the lead. We walk through a farmyard which could just as easily be a junkyard; farmers might be the gatekeepers of the countryside but some of them aren't half messy. Grobbelaar, Howard. Nothing for I. Great clumps of meadowsweet either side of the path. Jennings, Kahn, Lehmann, Maier, nothing for N, nothing for O. A proper track by the name of Clogger Lane, then a cattle-grid. Nothing for P, nothing for Q, Rimmer, Shilton, Trautmann. Climbing again, and a good view of Pendle Hill, Lancashire's very own Ayers Rock, or Uluru, shouldn't we say. Nothing for U. Van der Sar. Then the oddly named Cripple Hole Hill leading to the oddly named Robert Wilson's Grave. Who was Robert Wilson? Answer: Bob – goalkeeper for Arsenal, thank you. And so on and so forth, until Yashin, and last but not least, Zoff.

It could be coincidence, to do with walking under the hem of a cloud and feeling the sudden coldness of its shadow, but climbing Elslack Moor there's a definite sense of leaving the North Riding behind and heading into the West. And it feels like a true distinction, not just a crossing from one administrative region to another over an invisible line, but a sudden and perceptible change in atmosphere and environment, leaving those picturesque villages with their commemorative benches and placid duck ponds and entering somewhere altogether damper, higher and chillier, a transition from pastureland and enclosed fields to the scrubby upland and bare moors that I recognise as my home turf. Limestone seems to harbour an internal luminescence which lends a natural brightness to the Dales, but the gritstone here insists on something darker, as does the grey sky overhead and the ominous presence of Bradford and Leeds just over the next line of hills. The mills are largely demolished or converted into apartments, and the chimneys only stand as monuments to long-gone heavy industries, but through their roots the gloomy heathers and drab grasses seem to tap into the region's smoggy, soot-blackened history.

With every mile the light falters, and the temperature falls, and house prices drop.

By Lothersdale Slug's had enough, and so have I if I'm honest, but the pub isn't open, and a couple of seven-year-old lads skateboarding down the middle of the main road point to a gap in the wall where a footbridge crosses the river. There's a hill. Then another hill. Then another one. All right, not hills exactly but gradients all the same, and after fourteen miles of rambling through relatively flat and gentle countryside, any unanticipated incline feels like Kilimanjaro, not to mention a bloody impertinence. We're heading for Kirsten and Chris's terraced house, and only find it because Chris is standing in the middle of the lane waiting for us, along with another man who is taking lots of photographs of my triumphant entry into Middleton, or perhaps Cowling, or maybe Ickornshaw, though he doesn't seem entirely sure which one is me and which one isn't me, so he takes a lot of photographs of Slug's triumphant entry as well, and Slug plays to the camera, waving and smiling in a poet-like manner.

In return for the reading of a poem, Kirsten and Chris had offered a cuppa, a piece of cake, use of the toilet/telephone plus any medical attention I might need, but have actually gone quite a bit further and laid on something of a spread. They've also laid on several of their neighbours and friends, who are sitting either side of the open-plan living area and seem to extend as far back as infinity, or at least as far as the kitchen. One man presses into my hand a cartoon drawing of an overweight Noel Gallagher in walking gear communing with a sheep, which I realise after a few moments is meant to be me. Another man offers to give me a book, possibly of his own poems, and looks crushed when I tell him I can't carry the extra weight. It feels like they've been waiting for me all day, lovely people who've gone to a lot of trouble and expense to make me feel welcome, and I can't help thinking that now I've arrived I must be something of a disappointment, with barely enough energy and social grace to say hello to everyone, let alone tell a fascinating literary anecdote or recite 'Albert and the Lion' with a knotted hanky on my head. 'Who's the other one?' I hear a woman whisper, pointing at Slug with the toe of her shoe, and the man next to her just shrugs his shoulders. To make things worse I read a poem called 'Gooseberry Season', which I had always thought of as a parable-style poem about a man whose crimes of selfishness and arrogance meet with a just and appropriate punishment, but which in these circumstances sounds little more than the misjudged tale of an innocent, wandering stranger brutally murdered by redneck hillbillies. I want things to be right, because Kirsten and Chris and their kaleidoscope of friends seem like my kind of people, and given another couple of beers I could probably rise to the occasion. But Glyn is sitting in the corner with his car keys in his hand and his coat on, mindful of his wife's venison stew reaching its climax in the oven several miles away, alongside Slug's specially procured nut roast or lentil bake. And not only has Glyn worked tirelessly organising tonight's reading, he is also the Bearer of the Tombstone, which in Top Trump terms is the boss card.

*

Sir Gawain sets out across the wild, lawless landscape of England with no map other than the stars and no specific location to aim for other than somewhere called the Green Chapel, to keep an appointment with a green knight who has promised to behead him with his impressive axe. Like the *Odyssey*, it's one of the great journey poems, and like Odysseus, Gawain has to overcome many obstacles and endure much hardship along the route. He battles with bulls, bears and wild boars, wrestles with serpents and snarling wolves, and is pursued by giants over high ground. He also tangles with wodwos, which are 'satyrs or trolls of the forest' according to Tolkien, a man who knew a thing or two about mythical woodland creatures, and who made one of the earliest transcriptions and translations of the poem. Ted Hughes's poem 'Wodwo', from his book of the same name, is a monologue by some form of zoomorphic beast not sure of its identity or its place in the world, though in a letter to his friend Daniel Huws in 1967 Hughes mischievously suggests that Wodwo is 'a false singular for Wodwos, which is an apocopated plural for Wodwoses, which is middle English for Orang Outan'. Gawain must face his destiny on New Year's Day so travels during wintertime, bedding down in absolute blackness under frozen waterfalls, the rain and blizzards piercing his armour and chain mail. Knowing how cold and wet I've been walking the hills in several layers of waterproof and windproof fabrics during British summertime it's uncomfortable to think of making any kind of journey in December dressed only in a metal suit. On the outside of his shield he sports the endless knot, the gold five-sided star which stands as a token of his virtue and faith and as a reminder of the code of honour he must live by as a Christian and a knight.

Gawain's ordeal is a self-imposed test of physical and psychological endurance, and it is a test that he fails, first by abusing the hospitality of his host in respect of some ill-gotten gains, and secondly, with his head on the block and the axe-blade falling towards his neck, by losing his nerve. In recognition of his failure, and as a mark of his humility, Gawain returns to Camelot promising to wear a green garter or sash across his body for the rest of his days, a practice which is subsequently adopted by all the knights of the Round Table, and which some say is incorporated into the iconography of the Most Noble Order of the Garter, Britain's highest chivalric honour. So in Gargrave Village Hall it is not for no reason, as they say, that I read from *Sir Gawain and the Green Knight*. I think I will complete the

Pennine Way: the end is only a few horizons away now, and barring giants, serpents and the odd orang-utan, it feels like only a matter of time till I go striding into Edale with my reputation as a walker confirmed once and for all. But on the social side of things I can't help feeling that I haven't quite lived up to expectations, or more particularly that I have taken more than I have given, as in the astonishing £545.78 (and ten francs) crammed into the bulging sock by 178 of the good people of Gargrave, in exchange for what – a few poems, a bow of the head, and goodbye. There's also a Pennine Way badge in the sock, in the shape of a shield, which I'm not entitled to yet, and maybe this is my green sash, to be worn on my rucksack for evermore, 'a sign that his honour was stained by sin'. The microphone isn't working so I have to shout. At the book-signing afterwards, an old farmer in a tweed jacket and a flat cap says to me, 'Son, tha looks buggered.'

Ickornshaw to Hebden Bridge

16 MILES

OS Explorer OL21 North Sheet/South

Friday 23 July

I wake early, and when I open the curtains, the window frames a square of pure blue sky. I'd given up on the summer. Discounted it as a possibility. So even though a few months of decent weather per year should be a right rather than a privilege, today feels like an unexpected bonus and a welcome surprise. I manage to launder more change at the pub; it must look as if I've been raiding piggy banks or breaking into parking meters, but the landlady at the Mason's Arms doesn't bat an eyelid when I heave a carrier bag full of money onto the bar and tip out several hundred pounds' worth of gold and silver coins. Slug is asleep in one of the outside rooms and I have to bang on the door till he emerges. He's still enthusiastic about the walk but is limping slightly and concerned about holding me up. I tell him not to worry, because much as I like him I can't let an injured friend jeopardise the project at this stage, and that if he does suffer some kind of catastrophic breakdown up on Keighley Moor I'll either put him out of his misery with as little pain as possible or leave him there with a KitKat and a whistle.

'Do you know that song "Two Little Boys" by Rolf Harris?' I ask him.

'Yes,' he says.

'Well forget it.'

*

We're picking up where we left off yesterday. About a dozen of us leave Middleton, or Cowling, perhaps, or maybe Ickornshaw, including Kirsten and Chris and their daughter Marie, with a cuddly toy under her arm and still in her pyjamas and dressing gown, who probably wonders why she's part of a group of people traipsing across fields and climbing over walls before breakfast. In a German accent infused with Yorkshire vowels, Kirsten points out the small terraced cottage with a plaque on the wall where Philip Snowden was born. The first and three times Labour Chancellor of the Exchequer, Snowden converted to the left after being asked to present a paper on the dangers of socialism. At some point in his parliamentary career he was also MP for Colne Valley, the constituency in which I grew up, and went on to sit in the House of Lords as a viscount. Snowden came from an austere Wesleyan and Temperance background, and was a teetotaller himself, but full of drive and dreams, and I have a personal, partisan interest in people who have taken on the world in their own unexpected way, having emerged from unremarkable dwellings on unspectacular Yorkshire hillsides. In fact I'm sleeping in one such house tonight, birthplace to one such person, but that's still sixteen miles and two moors away.

The Cowling contingent drop off one by one, Chris turning back with sleepy Marie over his shoulder, the amateur paparazzo from yesterday capturing my triumphal crossing of the A6068 before declining the hillside ahead to return home, and Kirsten offering her hand to say goodbye, but because she is from continental Europe and because I'm a modern man not discomforted by such cosmopolitan gestures I kiss her on both cheeks instead. And then I blush.

We are now a party of six, comprising history teacher and local historian Rob, Anna who has organised tonight's reading, her husband Johnny and their sheepdog Bet, the ailing Slug, and myself. The path goes through some galvanised sheep-wrangling contraptions then up alongside a series of sinister-looking sheds, which Rob thinks are not grouse-shooting huts but chalets of some type, to be enjoyed by the good people of Cowling. Why they would want to trudge half a mile out of their own village to sit in a creosoted cabin isn't clear to me, but I like the idea that a desolate Yorkshire moor should have its own version of beach huts, and there is in fact an area of moor just a mile or so further along the Pennine Way named on the map as The Sea. Landmarks along this stretch come in the form of stones, including the Maw Stone, the Cat Stone, Little Wolf Stones and Great Wolf Stones, and further over to the north-west, the Hitching Stone. Said to be Yorkshire's biggest boulder at over a thousand tons, it was flung here from Ilkley Moor by a witch, and has a hole all the way through it which, if blown at a time of national crisis, will summon King Arthur and the Knights of the Round Table from their graves (I made that last bit up but the witch thing is true, obviously). The other notable sight is the line of wind turbines above Oxenhope, latter-day foes to any would-be Don Quixote.

Johnny has 'given up on shoes' he tells me, when I ask him why he is walking barefoot. And not just given up on them for the purpose of this walk but generally, in life, or at least where circumstances allow. I walk behind him along a boggy length of path, watching the peat squelch and rise up around his heels, then follow his tracks across a line of causey paving, his footprints slender, naked and primitive-looking alongside the stamp of dirty big walking boots. To 'feel' more of the walk Anna has also given up on shoes, and doesn't seem at all bothered by the thick mud and squashed sheep pellets oozing between her toes. Across the summit of the moor we must look like a line of Hare Krishna followers. All we need are the orange hoodies and a couple of bells.

This moor has a nightmare reputation in bad weather, both for getting lost and getting wet, but the weather today is glorious – clear and bright and still. Charles catches us up at Crag Top, Charles being the supplier of ecologically acceptable walking clothes including the top made from recycled wood chippings, which as luck would have it I happen to be wearing. I'd inadvertently given him the wrong starting position for today's walk (Ickornshaw, instead of Cowling, maybe, or possibly Middleton) but he's picked up our trail and jogged across the moor to hunt us down, puzzled by the combination of modern boot tread, dog-paw imprints and the footsteps of Yorkshire aborigines. At a nearby farm there are two visual treats, the first being an albino peacock, which strikes me as a near-perfect contradiction in terms, the second being a blue-and-white original Dormobile parked on a front lawn. A Dormobile is camping without a tent, holidaying without having to unpack, taking your living room for a drive; you'd have to have a heart of stone not to love a Dormobile or dream of sleeping under the concertina awning, and Slug has to take me gently by the elbow to ease me out of my Dormobile trance and guide me back onto the path, the path which plunges from Crag Top to Crag Bottom down the eastern side of Dean Clough via fields, driveways and a couple of gardens, then promenades along the far side of Ponden Reservoir before veering abruptly south, then west, rising towards the next expanse of moor.

The fact that Pennine Way signs are now appearing in both English and Japanese is an indication that we are entering Brontë country, and the fact that we are meeting some very casually dressed walkers, in sandals and Hawaiian shirts, for example, implies that we are now on part of a tourist trail. Thousands, quite possibly tens of thousands of people make the pilgrimage to Top Withens (or Withins, as it appears on the map) every year, many of them clutching copies of *Wuthering Heights*, some even clutching Kate Bush albums, and clamber among the ruins, or sit in the stone 'chair' hoping for some kind of spiritual or emotional connection with those astonishing sisters and their astonishing work. But for all that the town of Haworth has become the worldwide headquarters of the Brontë industry, the cobbled Main Street being a theme park of Brontë cafes and Brontë teapots and Brontë shortbread, Top Withens remains resolutely non-commercial, just a ruined farmhouse with a fallen-in roof and tumbledown walls. Even the carved plaque, set into the gable end by the Brontë Society in 1964, reads as a series of apologies, qualifying statements and outright disclaimers, with such phrases as 'has been associated with', 'may have been in her mind', and the altogether unequivocal 'bore no resemblance to'. Rather huffily, and as if it was written by the same person who provided similar signs for the houses of the Tooth Fairy, Father Christmas and the Easter Bunny, it ends: 'This plaque has been placed here in response to many inquiries.'

It's a good place for a picnic, though, with shelter and shade and stunning views to the south. A ram takes a bit of a shine to Slug, or rather to the sandwiches in his trouser pocket, and we take several compromising photographs of the ensuing coming together of man and sheep, and several Japanese visitors follow suit, all armed with expensive cameras and powerful, all-seeing lenses.

The flight of reservoirs at Walshaw Dean is low on water. Wherever all the rain of the past couple of weeks has been going it isn't here; Alcomden Water, the stream below the last dam wall, is little more than a trickle, and the exposed valley looks rusty and sore, with cracks opening along the banks of baked mud, and red and orange boulders littering the crusted basin. Anna has trodden on something sharp and is bleeding, and Slug is limping, so we're a little bedraggled and out of step by the time we round Standing Stone Hill, heading towards the ancient and cobbled village of Heptonstall. Like familiar chess pieces positioned across the arc of the distant horizon I can make out several regional landmarks, such as the phallic column of Stoodley Pike, the masts of Emley Moor, Pole Moor and Holme Moss, even Thurstonland Church, and the series of power stations leading out towards the east coast, Ferrybridge, Eggborough, Drax, their cooling towers pumping out vertical clouds of silver-white steam. Which means I'm nearing my own territory now, preparing for home.

Lower down, where the vegetation thickens, Johnny points out a few stands of Himalayan balsam, the new public enemy number one on the botanists' list of invasive species. In times gone by, Japanese knotweed was always the most wanted, and at one point was classified as a notifiable infestation. We had a big clump at the bottom of the garden which my dad would scythe down every year, but twelve months later it would be there again, taller and stronger. To try to stifle it he laid a square of heavy shag-pile carpet over the stalks, but they grew under it, around it and eventually through it. On one occasion he even resorted to a scorched-earth policy, tipping kerosene into the soil and setting fire to it, but nothing short of a US air strike and several barrels of napalm would have made any difference. In the end he settled for a partial truce or stalemate, and from his living-room window at the height of the summer I can still see the distinctive, heart-shaped leaves waving from the far end of the garden. The Himalayan balsam doesn't seem as deeply rooted – I pull a couple out as I'm wandering along and they come away easily – but according to Johnny they're taking over, and Johnny knows about these things.

Having been invited for a cup of tea and a lump of cake we call in at Lumb Bank, one of the Arvon Foundation's residential writing centres perched on a ledge above Colden Clough with a view down the narrow valley towards Hebden Bridge, and tiptoe past several students in gazebos, in the field, under fruit trees and dotted around the bee-bole garden, some with laptops and some with pads of paper, all deep in contemplation, all fighting with words. Strictly speaking the Pennine Way doesn't actually pass through Hebden Bridge, or the next town east along the bottleneck valley which is Mytholmroyd, but that's where I'm staying tonight, in one of those ordinary houses in an everyday street, not at all unlike the house I grew up in. Number 1 Aspinall Street is a back-to-back end-terrace with a lamppost outside. A few years ago it was acquired by the Elmet Trust, and is open to the public as well as being available for holiday lets. Mytholmroyd isn't an obvious tourist destination and Aspinall Street isn't exactly the golden mile, being one of several stone-built rows in a quiet residential area behind the busy A646 and beyond the dark and sluggish Rochdale Canal. But Ted Hughes was born at number 1, and even though he only lived there for the first six or seven years of his life, the view from the attic window and his experience of the neighbouring woods and cloughs gave rise to many of his most famous poems and provided a psychological, social and environmental template which was to serve his writing for the rest of his years.

On the wall between the front door (the only door, in fact) and the living-room window there's a blue plaque. I

know this because several years ago I stood on a makeshift
wooden podium and pulled a cord which drew back a pair
of little red curtains to reveal it, then made a short speech to
the gathering of friends, family and reporters, while a man
with dreadlocks and an acoustic guitar slung over his back
came marching through the proceedings, muttering under
his breath, clearly not daunted by the authoritative gleam of
Councillor Conrad Winterburn's mayoral chain, and quite
probably incensed by it. So I've stepped across the threshold
of this house quite a few times, but never slept in it, and
have been fantasising about spending the night in the
converted roof space which was Hughes' bedroom, gazing
up at the stars, and maybe even writing a poem. Staying
here is something exceptional and personal, something I've
been walking towards, wider than Malham Cove, taller
than High Force, deeper than High Cup Nick, an experience
that cannot be compromised or negotiated or shared.

'You're very uptight,' says my wife, when she arrives.

'I don't think Daddy wants us here,' says my daughter.

''Course I do.'

'Where's Slug?'

'Gone to Hebden Bridge to look for somewhere to stay.'

'Why can't he stay here? There's a spare bedroom.'

'Well I . . . er . . .'

'How is he getting to Hebden Bridge?'

'Walking.'

'Hasn't he got a bad leg?'

'The thing is . . .'

'Simon, you're very uptight.'

'I don't think Daddy wants us here.'

'I DO want you here and I'm NOT UPTIGHT, OK?'

We wander slowly up the road to the Ted Hughes Theatre at Calder High School, where Johnny goes past in a collared shirt and jacket, and Anna, checking tickets at the door, has made a Cinderella-like transformation and is now wearing a smart evening dress. Both of them are wearing shoes. Every day, during the walk, I think about the readings: where, when, which poems and in what order, who to thank, if anyone will attend. Then all the way through the readings I think about the walk: changing the map, charging the phone, checking the route, filling the water bottles, packing the Tombstone, applying the ointments. Anna says, 'The mayor was going to come but he's had his car stolen.' About two hundred people have made it, though that's a guess, because I'm too tired to remember to count. Neither can I remember what I read, because I'm on autopilot, somewhere else, having an out-of-body experience in which my body is sorting out clean socks and sandwiches for tomorrow while my mouth spouts poetry. The only time I make contact with myself is when I stumble over a word and have to reset the controls, or when my mind goes completely blank and I nod off at the wheel, then wake up suddenly with the reading veering into a ditch. I know that person on the front row, but who is it? Have I read here before? I opened this theatre, didn't I, or was that somewhere else? Am I a member of the Elmet Trust, or its patron? Or its president? Am I Ted Hughes?

By the time we get back to the house it's late. My daughter goes in the attic but comes back down saying she is 'freaked out up there', so we all end up in the same bed, and by four in the morning I'm tired of fighting for the sheets and being elbowed in the ribs, so I plod downstairs, make a cup of tea and tip out the sock on the kitchen table. Out slides a whopping £516.15, plus a slice of clingwrapped fruit cake, plus a photocopied and folded page from Ted Hughes's manuscript of his unfinished translation of *Sir Gawain and the Green Knight*, plus a piece of tree bark. I'm exhausted, and part of me never wants to read another poem in my life, let alone write one. But there's a soft, enticing, almost insistent dawn light radiating through the curtains and around the slats in the blind, and the first birds are beginning to call, and it's now or never. So with a notebook and a pencil I go back upstairs, and carry on going up, quietly, towards the very top of the house.

Above Ickornshaw, Black Huts

are raised against damp
on footings of red brick,
landlocked chalets lashed to the bedrock

with steel guy-ropes
and telegraph wire,
braced for Atlantic gales.

All plank and slat,
the salvaged timbers
ooze bitumen

out of the grain, a liquorice sweat,
its formaldehyde breath
disinfecting the clough

for a mile downwind.
Seen from distance,
these tarred pavilions or lodges

make camp on the ridge
in silhouette – black, identical sheds
of identical shape,

though up close
no two are alike,
being customised shacks,

a hillbilly hotchpotch
of water-butts, stoops,
a one-man veranda,

a stove-pipe wearing a tin hat.
And all boarded shut,
all housing

a darkroom darkness,
with pin-hole light
falling on nail or hook

or a padlocked box,
coffin-shaped, coiled
in a ship's chain.

Mothballed stations on disused lines
neither mapped nor named.
Birds avoid them –

some say the hatches fly open
and shotguns appear, blazing
at tame grouse,

that inside
they're all whisky and smoke,
all Barbour and big talk,

but others whisper
that locals sit here
in deckchairs, with flasks,

watching the dunes of peat,
binoculars raised,
waiting for downed airmen

or shipwrecked souls
to crawl
from the moor's sea.

Hebden Bridge to Marsden

14 MILES
OS Explorer OL21 South Sheet, OL1 West

Saturday 24 July

I once gave a reading in a small, modern, city-centre art gallery. At some point during the evening I noticed that members of the audience were nudging each other and tittering, and when I eventually glanced backwards, over my shoulder, I saw a man in a doughnut costume on the street outside, leaning against the glass wall and listening through the window. I then saw the house manager for the evening go out of the venue, and a minute or so later could hear him remonstrating with the doughnut, as could the rest of the audience. The conversation went something like this:

House manager: 'Excuse me, what do you think you're doing?'

Doughnut: 'I'm a doughnut.'

House manager: 'So I see. Do you have to stand here?'

Doughnut: 'I'm advertising doughnuts. It's my job.'

House manager: 'We've got a poetry reading going on in there.'

Doughnut: 'So what, doughnuts can like poetry.'

A car went past and I didn't catch the next few words, but then heard the manager say, 'Well, why don't you come inside?' Although I was reading a poem from the page in front of me, my mind was actually saying, 'Don't bring the doughnut into the reading, please don't bring the doughnut into the reading.' The doughnut then said to the house manager, 'I can't, I'm waiting for a colleague.' I don't remember what happened next, except for thinking that if TWO doughnuts came inside, I would put down my book and retire.

The incident made me very wary of reading in any venue where the outside world can look in. Places like Standedge Tunnel and Visitor Centre, a cavernous, open-plan former boatshed with tall glass doors. Behind me, as I launch into the first poem, I can sense latecomers and nosey parkers pressing their faces to the glass and hear them rattling the handles and locks. At the far end, through an equally big window, dog-walkers and bike riders stop to peer in. With fifty-six people seated in narrow rows in front of me, I'm sitting on the metal steps trying to compete with another voice – my own – as it echoes between the girders and rattles around the stone walls. I prefer to stand when I read, but I'm already several feet above the audience, and it's good to take the weight off. The steps have yellow lines painted onto them to stop people missing their footing, and the arched stone entrance that frames me is flanked by floor-to-ceiling ironwork; to all outward appearances I am reading in the wing of a Category A prison. It's supposed to be the climax, the wandering minstrel at his homecoming gig, but it doesn't work. They say you can't be a priest in your own parish, and maybe that adage applies to poets as well. Many people in the audience are friends or family, or the friends of family, and they've heard it all before. Slug has certainly heard it all before, in Grasmere, Malham, Gargrave, Hebden Bridge, and now again in Marsden. I've tried to vary it, but it's only ever a variation on a theme, and choosing which poems to read has become like choosing from set-menu options in a Chinese restaurant, tonight being menu C: 'The Shout', 'Causeway', 'Roadshow', followed by 'You're Beautiful', 'The Christening', Sweet and Sour Chicken, Crispy Duck, Egg Fried Rice and fresh lychees for dessert. Every time a train goes past on the westbound line it sounds its horn before entering the three-mile tunnel, like some kind of poetry censoring system, bleeping words, phrases and sometimes whole sentences.

Afterwards, someone has set up a book stall in the children's play area. I hang my jacket over one of the tiny chairs, sit with my knees up by my ears, and sign a few copies. In the pub across the road there's a celebratory atmosphere. Slug buys a bottle of cava to toast my achievement, then the drinks are on me, or rather they are on the £110.18 in the sock, which also contains a scented candle and (a recurring theme by now) a packet of Elastoplast. I should let my hair down a bit, get drunk with the rest of them, but I can't, partly out of being sensible (and uptight etc.) and partly out of guilt, because even though I have walked home I have not yet completed the Pennine Way, and tomorrow I have to set off again, drag myself up to Brun Clough Reservoir by eight in the morning and haul my sorry arse over very horrible Black Hill, and the day after that, find my way across the even more horrible Bleaklow and Kinder Scout, on my own. When the Apollo 13 mission went wrong, the astronauts had to bypass the Earth and make a momentum-building slingshot around the dark side of the Moon, and watched helplessly as the blue planet sailed past the window of their spacecraft. That might seem like an exorbitant metaphor for someone who only has to overshoot his own house by twenty-seven miles, and the Peak District isn't exactly the final frontier. But sitting in the pub with the glasses clinking around me and another bottle of bubbly arriving in a plastic bucket, I can't help but feel a bit of a fraud, and that all this rejoicing is somewhat premature. The name of the pub is the Tunnel End, the end of the tunnel being the place where light is. And that's still two days away.

*

Twelve hours earlier we'd convened above Lumb Bank, a new party for another day, being the three Armitages, my friend Rick, making a reappearance after an impressive performance between Dufton and Langdon Beck, and his wife Jo. But not Slug, who has thrown in the towel, and whose non-appearance this morning has absolutely nothing whatsoever to do with a former girlfriend who happens to live in the Hebden Bridge area, he insists. He will 'follow on by public transport', and his place is taken by the last-minute arrival of Subhadassi, who spotted me last year in the basement jumble sale of Huddersfield's TK Maxx store, came alongside and said, 'So is this where poets buy their jackets?' Subhadassi ('a glimpse of beauty') was born in Huddersfield and ordained a Buddhist in Spain in the early nineties. His other conversion was from chemistry to the arts; amongst other things he's a fine poet and an entertaining walking companion. It must take some courage to turn up and walk with someone you've only met for a few seconds in the men's section of an 'off-price retailer', and must also take some courage to be a Huddersfield-born Buddhist going by the name Subhadassi.

'You can call me Paul,' he tells me.

'No, Subhadassi's cool,' I say, rather naffly, though already I'm anticipating a rendezvous with my dad later in the day, and wondering just how cool he will be when I introduce him to someone from Yorkshire who isn't called Fred or Jim.

*

After winding its way down the valley side, intricately navigating various cobbled pathways, meandering through private gardens and in front of mullioned windows, the Pennine Way crosses the A646, the Rochdale Canal, the River Calder and the Halifax–Manchester railway line just west of Charlestown, then zigzags through Callis Woods and around Lodge Hill until Stoodley Pike Monument appears in the distance. From several miles away the Pike looks, well, monumental, a proud and flawless sculpture, obsidian black even in bright sunlight, like something out of ancient Egypt. Up close, though, it's a disappointment, the colossal stone blocks weathered and soot-stained, the tower a four-cornered obelisk rather than the smoothly formed cone it appeared to be from further away, the internal staircase urine-scented and uninviting, so much so that I don't bother to climb it. It was originally built to com-memorate the defeat of Napoleon, then collapsed due to lightning damage, has been restored twice, and now appears to commemorate many a local vandal, several courting couples and an ardent supporter of Manchester City, the scratched and spray-painted graffiti speaking far louder than the letter-carved plaque. But it isn't necessary to climb the tower to enjoy the view, which is pretty much panoramic, or to find somewhere to picnic, after which I suggest we press on – the wind's getting up and we're not even halfway.

Along the banks of Warland Reservoir Subhadassi tells me he thinks I'm doing a modern-day *Poly-Olbion*, Michael Drayton's seventeenth-century topographical poem, being a '*CHOROGRAPHICALL DESCRIPTION OF ALL THE TRACTS, RIVERS, MOUNTAINS, FORESTS, and other Parts of this Renowned Isle of GREAT BRITAIN, with intermixture of the most Remarkeable Stories, Antiquities, Wonders, Rarities, Pleasures, and Commodities of the same.*' Just as he's describing Drayton's all-encompassing, versified gazetteer of the British Isles with its woodland nymphs and sprites of the streams, the hills over his right shoulder open like curtains, and Greater Manchester comes steaming into view, from Rochdale just below us to Stockport in the south to Bolton in the north, a great urban bay, and the first city I've seen for the best part of three weeks. The further we walk the more immense it becomes, until it isn't just part or even most of the view, but pretty much all of it. It seems implausible, incongruous, even anachronistic, and yet inevitable, something that couldn't be held off or ignored any longer. All this time I've been walking down the middle of a remote wilderness with wide buffer zones of unpopulated hills and uninhabitable moor to either side, but this hulking municipal mass means that I'm getting closer to the edge, and nearer to the end. I pull my cap down diagonally so the peak acts as a one-sided blinker, and keep my eyes to the floor. The next time I look up it's because there's a little old man standing in front of me, blocking the path, his arm extended, wanting to shake me by the hand.

'Are you Simon Armitage?'

'Yes.'

'Ha! I don't believe it!' he says. 'That's two of you now. I met Seamus Heaney last week!'

'*He's* not doing the Pennine Way, is he?'

'He was in a pub,' he says, then, 'Unbelievable!' Then he spins on his heel and disappears, leaving me with the thought of walking into the Old Nag's Head in Edale in a couple of days' time only to find Heaney sitting at the bar having got there first, Amundsen to my Scott, the story already told, the book already written.

*

Whichever pub Heaney was in he isn't at the White House, where the Pennine Way crosses the A58, but my dad is.

'Who's the other feller?' he whispers.

'Subhadassi.'

'Who?'

'Subhadassi.'

'Shirley Bassey?'

'Pack it in, Dad.'

'Sub-a-bloody-dassi? Where's he from?'

'Huddersfield.'

'Aye, it's a good old Yorkshire name is that. What's he do?'

'He's a poet.'

'Well that explains it. Has he got a proper job?'

This sketch carries on until Subhadassi has unlaced his boots in the porch, shaken my dad by the hand and offered to buy him a drink. 'Seems like a decent bloke, any road,' my dad concedes, still scratching his chin but having ordered a pint of bitter.

After a personnel exchange – my mum substituted for my daughter, who has pointed out that 'it wouldn't be fair to let Grandad drive home on his own' – we cross the main road and scramble up towards Blackstone Edge, via the allegedly Roman Road and the curious Aiggin Stone, a crudely cut and cryptically coded waymarker. Chamfered towards the bottom, the stone is prone to occasional swooning fits; having fallen over on at least two occasions during the 1970s it was returned to the vertical by concerned parties, and currently stands at an angle of about eighty degrees.

The person responsible for giving Blackstone Edge its name could never be accused of hyperbole, it being one of the bleakest and most barren features on the whole of the Pennine Way, and I don't say this as a mean-spirited Yorkshireman scoring a cheap point simply because the path has veered momentarily into Lancashire. And perhaps it's just the contrast with the structured and glowing limestone of Malham Cove, but geology appears to have crash-landed here, with dark and broken stone lying dumped and abandoned in unlovely heaps and piles. The scars and exposed rocks on the lower hillside are all the product of human quarrying, but up here the weather is the excavator, scalping the turf then scouring and sculpting the stone beneath. The actual path disappears for a while, having been blown away or fallen down one of the crevices, then rematerialises a few hundred yards later on the boulder-littered plateau, requiring some smart footwork to negotiate. The view, I admit, is incredible, stretching way beyond the sprawling conurbation of Greater Manchester as far as the west coast and the Welsh mountains and the Great Orme. With the spinnaker of its high white dish standing tall and proud, Jodrell Bank radio telescope looks like an enormous yacht sailing across the Cheshire plain. But there's only so much sharp, cold light the eyeballs can take up here, and there are dark clouds ganging up to the south.

Like the A66 all those days ago, the M62, when we reach it, seems absurd, with uncountable vehicles travelling at insane speeds across an otherwise empty and unconquered moor. Away to the east lies Scott Hall Farm; urban myth says that the farmer refused to budge when the motorway was being built, but revised opinion suggests that the carriageways had to divide in any event, due to the lie of the land. Still a working farm decades later, it's also the most famous central reservation in Britain, with cows passing through a subway en route to the milking shed each evening. I once met a man in Colne who sold a prize ram to the owner of Scott Hall Farm, a real beauty, apparently, with the perfect Roman nose, handsome face and exquisitely formed horns, and the ram was doing well up there at the side of the motorway until somebody pulled over one night and hacked off its head for a trophy. Subhadassi also has an M62 anecdote. Waiting on the bridge above it with his mother and a big crowd of people in 1971 to witness the official opening of that stretch of the motorway, he was peeing through the railings just as the Queen's Rolls-Royce came around the corner and passed underneath.

'What did your mother say?'

'She wasn't happy.'

I think it's fair to say that my own mother isn't very happy either at present, approaching the footbridge that spans the six lanes as if it were something made from creepers and vines slung across a jungle ravine. She's never been comfortable on anything higher than the bottom rung of a stepladder, and I watch her steeling herself for the crossing, then taking a centre line over the arched walkway, as far away from the edge as possible, elbows in, fists clenched. Somewhere near the middle, where the bridge sways slightly in the wind that funnels through the cutting below, in that sweet spot where the concrete vibrates and the metalwork quivers and sings as it reaches its resonant frequency, she closes her eyes.

The trig point of White Hill comes and goes. This degraded area of moorland is a Pennine Way black spot as far as bogs and peaty quagmires are concerned, but apart from a few problems at a place marked on the map as 'Fords', solved by a combination of stepping-stone construction, triple-jumping technique and a piggy-back rota, we all stay dry. Or at least until those black clouds finally arrive, and rain begins to fall, coinciding exactly with the first view of Marsden off to the left. Sixteen days ago I set off from Scotland, with the specific ambition of walking the whole of the Pennine Way, but with the more sentimental objective of making it back to the village I grew up in, to that part of the country which has such a strong claim on my identity, such an influence on my writing and such a pull on my life. There would be no shame in failing to reach Edale; I'm forty-seven years old, I spend a lot of time in a chair and I'd done little or no training. But after making such a palaver about the whole project, the idea of not making it to Marsden was mortifying, unthinkable. In fact the potential humiliation of falling short of that target was a built-in incentive, and to that end I'd anticipated an emotional and spiritual reunion of some kind, or at least some sense of perspective on the theme of 'home' having slogged halfway across the country to get here. But seeing the village coming into focus, the honest truth is that I feel very ordinary, even a little bit lost. I keep looking at the place names on the map then peering down the valley to my left, then checking my reaction, but there's nothing either high or low to report, neither the elation of re-entry nor the bump of coming back down to earth. I have walked home, so where is the thrill, or the sense of achievement, or the glow of pride?

As we plod towards the Dinner Stone and Thieves Clough I push forward on my own. To the rest of the group it probably looks like I'm being propelled along the final straight by a surge of adrenalin, or as if this moving homecoming is something I need to experience alone. But I'm simply embarrassed about my lack of reaction and want to keep it to myself. Or I need to understand it, and with the familiar bald head of Pule Hill just half a mile away now the only explanation I can think of is this: that I'm a creature of habit. Yes I like journeys, an excursion every now and again, the occasional expedition and even an odd adventure once in a while, but at the end of the day I'm very happy with the way things are, or rather *where* things are. Which is why, presumably, I'm still living three miles from the hospital I was born in. And why I wanted to tackle the Pennine Way, which would return me to my front door, and why I wanted to do it the wrong way round – to get back to all that is comfortable and familiar, everything I call home. But over the past fortnight, my habitat has become the journey itself and my new habit is to walk. That's what I do now: I lace up my boots and head into the hills, then do the same again the next day, and the day after that, and the day after that. Where do I live at the moment? On the move. It's a routine, a rhythm, the norm. I walk therefore I am. And now that I've got used to it, I feel too lazy to stop.

I can see my dad's car in the car park, where we've arranged to meet, and pipe smoke drifting out of the open window. The rain begins to pour, and I turn around just in time to see my mum producing a plastic recycling sack out of her bag and pulling it over her head.

Marsden to Crowden

12 MILES

OS Explorer OL1 West Sheet

Sunday 25 July

However, after a night in my own house and in my own bed, and after taking a bath in my own bath and washing my hair with my own shampoo, I've remembered which habits I'm *really* a creature of, so it's with extreme reluctance, both mental and physical, that I make my way back to Standedge and pull down my hood against the raging wind. Martyn Sharp, Pennine Way Ranger, Peak District National Park, might have been just as reluctant to give up his Sunday and nursemaid a poet across his place of work, but if he was, he's good enough not to say so. We hang around for ten minutes or so, waiting for three strangers who had threatened to walk with me but who fail to show up, then set off up the slabbed section of path that bisects Black Moss and Swellands Reservoirs then arcs left into Wessenden Valley. To say that I know this area like the back of my hand is probably an overstatement (not to mention a cliché, although presented with the backs of several hands to choose from, would I really be able to pick out my own? I once saw the back of my hand on a 'visualiser', a high-power projector which throws an image of the magnified object onto a big screen, and it didn't look like a writer's hand at all but the hand of some rough, filthy cave-dweller), but I know it well enough, having wandered across these moors on hundreds of occasions, sometimes nature-watching or on sponsored walks, sometimes with family and friends having a bit of a ramble, but mainly alone with no special reason or specific purpose. Right from being a boy I was quite happy strolling around on the hills, and quite happy if someone came with me, though I preferred it when they didn't. It's what my dad had done as a child, and his descriptions of the moors as endless, empty and ungoverned places where a person could go wherever they wanted and not see a soul all day made me want to follow suit. In the years before more organised and packaged forms of recreation, he even brought us up here on holiday. It was a trip of no more than two miles from our front door and a vacation with no actual focus or plan of action other than *to be here*, and after pitching a heavy canvas tent at the side of some shallow lake or stream then firing up the little Calor Gas stove and breaking open a tin of soup, we'd stroll around looking for entertainment and action, largely in the form of water or stones. Good times.

When I started to think about this walk I had an image in my mind of my dad coming with me today, walking back across the hills where he'd roamed as a youngster, accompanying me to the village boundary and seeing me over the horizon. My mother walking me in, my father walking me out. But he's more comfortable in the driving seat of a car these days, with New Orleans jazz pumping through the speakers and his pipe in his mouth, and tends to reserve his energy for the bowling green, either playing on it (a game he once dismissed as 'old men's marbles' but now seems addicted to) or cutting it, following the petrol-driven mower up and down then back and across, striping the surface into a jade-coloured tartan. I look down to where the bowling green is a lush oasis among many square miles of drab grasses, but he isn't there. Still in bed, probably, thinking about getting up and peeling the potatoes before Mum gets back from church. Or he'll have gone for the Sunday papers, a journey of about three hundred yards, or two minutes in the car.

Situated at the head of a valley and no stranger to rainfall, one of Marsden's primary functions over the centuries has been to gather water; to service the region's industries, to slake the thirst of its population, and to top up the canals. Consequently, most true Marsdeners are word-perfect when it comes to reeling off the names of those reservoirs and lakes lying in elevated isolation somewhere above their heads. If they forget, they can always pop into the Riverhead Brewery, whose hand-pumped beers are christened in honour of those reservoirs, and order a pint of Butterley or Red Brook or March Haig. (That said, since the pub found itself to be an integral part of a railway-based 'ale trail', shuttling between Dewsbury on one side of the Pennines to the public bar on Stalybridge Station on the other, they might have to run the gauntlet of large groups of amiably pissed middle-aged men carrying well-thumbed copies of the *Good Beer Guide* and wearing grass skirts.) Butterley is fed by Blakeley Reservoir, which is fed by Wessenden, which is fed by Wessenden Head. The Pennine Way, which rises through the valley alongside them, is a vehicle track as far as the deer farm at Wessenden Lodge, and a rough path thereafter, or a 'pitched path' as Martyn calls it, where large stones are set into the ground on end, so the part we walk on is just the tip of the iceberg, as it were. I notice yellow-and-black snails, like old-fashioned humbugs, clinging to the underside of fern leaves, and it's going to be strange walking anywhere ever again without meadow pipits springing up from underfoot. A thick, woolly caterpillar writhes and rolls on the face of a flat, warm stone, and a few yards later, an even thicker, woollier one throws the same moves.

As Saddleworth Moor opens up to the right, conversation turns to the Hindley and Brady murders, and to the unrecovered body of Keith Bennett, still said to be buried in a shallow grave somewhere in that bleak expanse of open ground. Martyn remembers a zip fastener being found in a peat bog some years ago, and a solitary policeman having to stand guard over it all night until a forensics team arrived in the morning. I can't think of many worse places, or worse circumstances, in which to be alone in the dark, and the story strikes me as the sinister obverse of Adrian's anecdote about the round-the-clock protection of the lady's slipper orchid near Malham Tarn. The moor is bisected by the exposed and precarious A635, known locally as the Isle of Skye road because of the legendary Isle of Skye public house which once stood at the eastern end of the crossing. Black Hill looms up ahead, with a shimmering line of damp paving stones stretching towards it, like a sacred pathway leading to a Mayan temple or some site where slaughter and sacrifice might have taken place. The slabs are reclaimed from the floors of Lancashire mills and helicoptered in three or four at a time, then levered into position by hardy volunteers or by Martyn, who once got a ride in the chopper but didn't get to play with the controls. Many of the slabs still bear the scars of their former industry, such as the grooves, bolts, hinges and anchor points which held the machines of the cotton trade in place, and the rough undersides are usually turned face up, to give traction to the boots of those who now walk on them. The slabs are put in place at considerable expense and as a most welcome courtesy, and those who oppose their presence should relax and take a longer, evolutionary perspective on the subject, because the moor will swallow the paving stones eventually, just as it absorbs and digests everything else that attempts to stake a position here.

Where degradation and depletion of the surface has become more widespread, sheep have been fenced out, and I spot two rowan-tree saplings which have taken root under a south-facing bank, and the beginnings of a silver birch. For lunch, we drop behind an open trench and use the solid wall of peat behind us as backboard, feeling the heat stowed in its dense crust, watching a couple of big brown hares lolloping about on the far side of Issue Clough. I can see my house from here, but that isn't such a surprise because I can see just about EVERYONE'S house from here, the much-quoted statistic being that the next highest point going east is the Ural Mountains in Russia. Whenever someone calls him, Martyn's phone plays a ring-tone version of 'Sold England' by the Levellers, and I get a text from my wife to say she's found Slug in our garden with a pair of scissors in his hand standing next to a privet bush in the shape of a chipmunk with a Mohican.

Black Hill stands at 581 metres, with the nipple of Soldier's Lump standing a little higher, constructed by the Ordnance Survey many moons ago to house a theodolite. There's also a more familiar-looking white trig point on the summit which, because the hill is sinking under its own weight, has been hoisted up on a dry-stone plinth. Martyn helped build it, and threw a wine bottle into the cavity to celebrate its creation before sealing it up.

'White or red?'

'Red.'

There are twenty, maybe even thirty elderly walkers milling around on the summit in the mist, drinking tea and comparing biscuits, so busy in their gossiping that they barely notice us as we steer south and begin our long, gradual descent. The area we pass through now is known as Red Ratcher, presumably because of the open wounds of blood-coloured streams which stripe the hillside, whose rusty-looking, oxidised waters pour across the path and stain the rocks. Martyn makes a note of a section of the route which could do with paving, but says it's hard to entice gangs of flaggers out into the middle of the moors when for the same lolly they could be mending pavements in Doncaster. I know where I'd rather be. We watch a dog running wild on the other side of the valley, a springer spaniel, and Martyn says the local farmer will shoot it if he sees it.

'Is he a shoot-first-ask-questions-later sort of person?'

'Just a shoot-first person. No questions.'

As if we have passed into bandit country, Martyn then tells me about having the bobcat stolen one night (the bobcat being a sort of quad bike-cum-moon buggy, very useful when working on these hills), and about sheep rustling, and about the Snake Pass as the major drug-running corridor between Sheffield and Manchester. To add to the atmosphere we step over the carcass of a disembowelled lamb, and a few yards later a dead pigeon, its breast exposed, minus its head and feet, probably taken out by a peregrine. When I was a child, the allotments and back gardens all along the lower slopes of the moor held many dozens of black-and-white-painted pigeon lofts, full of fidgeting and flapping birds, purring with noise whenever I walked past them, like mini generators or sub-stations. I never got into it myself but some of my school friends spent every spare minute with their fathers or grandfathers locked inside those huts, or I'd see them setting off in the car with a hamper full of live birds in the back, or standing outside the lofts with binoculars and stopwatches, scanning the skies. Tales circulated of birds changing hands for thousands of pounds, and pigeons that had made it back from as far away as the Balkans, or had been given up for dead only to come tumbling home several weeks later having walked the last few miles. In that world, raptors were the enemy, and peregrine falcons the Luftwaffe.

But a dead pigeon near Black Chew Head could be thought of as a mere token or morbid emblem, because the skies overhead are clearly not safe, the Peak District being something of an aeroplane graveyard, with over sixty crash sites documented. In November 1948, an innocuous half-hour flight delivering payroll and mail from Lincolnshire to Warrington ended in catastrophe when a Boeing Superfortress with a crew of thirteen ploughed into Shelf Moor. The plane, 'Overexposed', which belonged to a photographic reconnaissance squadron and carried an image of a nude pin-up girl on its fuselage, is still scattered across the moor; torn and mangled engine parts lie slumped in the peat, and a lonely memorial stone nearby often stands decorated with paper poppies and draped in the Stars and

Stripes. 'You'll be walking past it tomorrow,' says Martyn, pointing towards Bleaklow to the south, before embroidering the historical facts with tales of a ghost plane which often flies through low cloud over these hills, and a headless pilot who staggers about in the mist and who has confronted several lone hikers over the years.

'Aren't you walking on your own tomorrow?'

'Yes.'

'What's the weather forecast?'

'Fog.'

*

Laddow Rocks is an impressive and unmistakable gritstone outcrop above Crowden Great Brook, and the path runs along the precipitous edge of the crag and close to several overhanging boulders, too close for my liking. Then it's all downhill to Crowden, with a party of Jewish schoolboys heading in the other direction, making no concession whatsoever in their choice of clothes to the great outdoors or the Great British weather. A seemingly endless line of them keeps filing past in sensible black shoes, white shirts and black waistcoats, their dark ringlets wet with sweat, cheeks red with the effort of climbing, their black velvet kippahs somehow staying in place on the crowns of their heads. Just when we think we've witnessed the last straggler or the out-of-condition teacher bringing up the rear, another pair appear, then another five or six, then more of them, like something from the Bible, all scrambling to the top of Laddow Rocks, all making for higher ground.

What do they know that we don't?

On their patio in Glossop, Lisa and Sean fatten me up with a Thai barbecue – 'the last supper' – then it's off to the last reading, which has been switched at the eleventh hour from Glossop North End Football Club to the Oakwood pub in the town due to bar-staffing problems, apparently. I'm anticipating a difficult night, reciting poetry to the disinterested, the disparaging and the drunk, but I couldn't be more wrong. The bouncers on the door are three ladies from a local bookshop, who lead me up the stairs to a private room with a stage and a glitter curtain at the far end. The room fills up, and up, and up, until ninety-one people are either leaning against the wall or sitting on the floor or perched on tables at the back, and for the next hour or so I

stand in a spotlight with a pint of beer at one side and a pile of books at the other and I ENJOY MYSELF, even smile a couple of times. With every poem I can feel my spirits rising, a weight lifting, and the burden of public performance evaporating by the second. In fact I give it EVERYTHING, even if 'everything' isn't much more than a very tired person standing with a book in front of his face, opening his mouth and making noises (some of which *do* in fact rhyme, though only occasionally and rarely at the end of the lines). As well as policing the door the bouncers/booksellers have been on sock duty for me, and hand over £215.58, plus sundry items including a teabag, a parking ticket, a pine cone, a dental appointment card (8 October, 3.15 p.m.), a playing card (Joker), and a mobile-phone number ('Brenda. Call me').

Then I'm done.

Crowden to Edale

15 MILES

OS Explorer OL1 West Sheet

Monday 26 July

Like the king of the world and the lord and master of all I survey, I am sitting on a flat rock eating a big lump of sugary cake and drinking black coffee from a flask, coffee infused with an intoxicating nip of single malt. It is a warm, clear afternoon with long views to the south and the east. Behind me is Kinder Scout and 250-odd miles of the Pennine Way; in front of me the steep gully and natural steps of Jacob's Ladder descend from the moor towards a broadening, green valley in the Derbyshire Peak District. And beyond that lies the sleepy community of Edale, like some toy village on children's TV, where animals drive cars and kindly old ladies ride penny-farthings and a relentlessly chirpy postman makes his rounds in a bright red van with his cat on the passenger seat. Smoke rises from behind a barn. A train leaves the station. By glancing down at the map then scanning the cluster of buildings I can just about figure out which is the church, and the visitors' centre, and the Old Nag's Head Inn, starting point for the Pennine Way, or in my case, the finishing post. In that pub resides what I imagine to be a leather-bound, gold-embossed, parchment-paged ledger, locked in a glass case, containing all the names of those heroes who have taken part in this great adventure, to which I will soon be adding my own. This is the last vista, the last elevation, and these minutes should be a time of contemplative satisfaction before the final easy miles, the concluding steps, and the chequered flag.

But I am not going to Edale. Over the past few days, and especially since the false dawn of arriving home in Marsden only to set off again, I've been wondering long and hard about how to end this journey, pondering the variables. Of course, on the face of it there are no variables, only one very obvious, inevitable and desirable course of action, which is to breast the tape, complete the task, and bask in the glory. But yesterday, walking between Standedge and Crowden, another outcome occurred to me, one that began as an insane and outrageous notion but grew in strength and conviction over the following miles, to the point where not only was it a viable alternative to the traditional ending, but in fact the only possibility. And here it is: I am not going to finish. My plan, instead, is one of deliberate refusal, a kind of self-sabotage which will take me to within a few strides of the finishing line only to see me turn around and head back into the hills. It's a dramatic gesture, theatrical even, but one based on a few honest principles, the first being that I am not interested in conquest for its own sake. I have walked the Pennine Way to prove myself – artistically, economically, physically, whatever – and I don't need a cup on the mantelpiece or a badge on my rucksack to put that success on display. This will be the triumph of personal accomplishment over public affirmation. I'm not about medals or trophies, or if I am, I need to rethink myself. Secondly, for as long as the walk remains unfinished I still have direction, and something to aim for, and somewhere to go. To start ticking off achievements as if they were rungs of attainment on the ladder of fulfilment would be to go against everything I have come to believe in as a person and a poet. Be careful what you wish for, especially if that thing is THE END. And thirdly, very possibly in contradiction with those high-minded values and studied philosophical positions just described, and whilst accepting that a long walk is not and never should be a competition and that victory is a shallow and embarrassing state of affairs, this is how I WIN. Because over the past three weeks the Pennine Way has done everything in its power to see me fail. It has laughed at me with the wind and pissed on me with the rain. It has lured me into thick fog, misdirected me through forests and woods, and abandoned me in the empty fells, leaving me to sigh and swear, and on at least one occasion, to weep. On flinty tracks it has beaten the soles of my feet and on softer ground tried to suck me into the earth. It has steered me close to resentful land-owners and placed undomesticated creatures beset with horns and teeth directly in my path. It has made the inclines seem steeper and the miles longer, and in more ways than one has toured me close to the edge and deep into the chasm. I have been embarrassed, spooked, exhausted, exposed, lonely, and I stink; in fact it has tried every trick in the book, but guess what – I'm still here.

So although the knee-jerk reaction would be to see it through and deliver the death blow, I won't give it the satisfaction of taking that final step, because the more dignified course of action is simply to turn around and walk away. This has been a big journey, but I'm even bigger, and anyone standing at the Old Nag's Head with streamers and balloons or even just a pint of best will be in for a long wait. I imagine all my forebears, the ones with medals on their chests and trophies in the cupboard, not understanding at all, throwing up their arms in disgust, disowning me as I spin on my heel and start walking north, but I don't care. There are a couple of escape routes around the village of Booth, I can hop over the wall and leg it across the fields onto the road, then thumb a lift back to Crowden where I left the car. Then I can slip away home, having had the prize offered to me on a plate and having happily turned it down.

That, at least, was the plan. But the reality goes something like this. I wake up in my own bed and pull the curtains back. The bedroom window has a big view over Honley and Holmfirth to the west, then across the fields and plantations around Yateholme reservoir, climbing to Black Hill and Saddleworth Moor and the Dark Peak. Those distant features aren't visible because a thick roll of cloud draws a line across the horizon at about four hundred metres, but it's still early, just one of those summer morning mists, and the forecast predicts it will clear. I shower, eat, read the paper, listen to the radio. There's no rush. I even drop my daughter off at school.

'I thought you were doing the Pennine Way,' says one of the mums.

'I am,' I say, gesturing towards my walking boots and my mud-stained trousers. On the other hand, I am several miles from the route and have just climbed out of a climate-controlled Volkswagen Passat, so I can see her point.

I drive over Holme Moss. There are still faint words written on the road from where the Milk Race used to climb out of Yorkshire then drop down into Derbyshire on the other side of the hill, and the car park at the top is one of those places where people come to enjoy the view on a Sunday without getting out of their vehicle. A few hundred yards away across the moor the flat-roofed, single-storey radio station looks uninviting and suspicious, the kind of place where messages are decoded, where experiments go unrecorded and secrets are kept. I have it in my head that someone I know has the unenviable job of climbing the mast in the winter to defrost the satellite dishes and hack blocks of ice from the transmitter, but I might have dreamt it. It's a bleak place, the touching point for three counties, with nowhere to escape the wind no matter which direction it blows from or how calm it seems in the valleys beneath. The snow poles on the even steeper valley on the west side of the hill tell their own story, as do the reinforced crash barriers above the drop, full of scrapes and dents and gaping holes. They also serve notice of another geography, one more dramatic and intense than the broad, elevated moorlands of West Yorkshire, higher and steeper, the last stumbling blocks and obstacles facing the hiker heading south, a final act of geological defiance before the Pennines dwindle into lowlands and plains. The Derbyshire Peaks, visible from Manchester on one side and Sheffield on the other, are a magnet for walkers, climbers, bird-spotters, mountain bikers, etc.; they are also, in my mind, synonymous with disappointment and despair.

I pull up in the visitors'-centre car park on the south shore of Torside, one of a flight of five reservoirs which effectively dam the whole of Longdendale and the River Etherow. If anything the cloud seems to have descended, and after a few minutes of trying to tune the radio into a weather forecast and studying the map I realise that I can't see the far side of the valley without flicking the windscreen wipers on and off. It's about 9.30; I've usually been walking for a good hour at this time, and I'm uncomfortable, embarrassed even at the loss of routine and the fall in standards on this final day. I'm nervous as well, because this is a treacherous stretch of hills, notoriously difficult to navigate and horribly wet underfoot. I've set out to cross them once before and failed, and for the first time in several days of walking I'm on my own, and the mist has now turned to fog, through which rain is falling, that type of rain which without actually pelting down somehow manages to be very wet. A further complication today is that I'm supposed to be meeting a couple of rangers from the National Trust at the top of Kinder Downfall to record a poem about cotton grass, which as far as I understand will be broadcast by my disembodied voice from a camouflaged speaker somewhere on a desolate hillside when triggered by unsuspecting hikers or puzzled sheep. It's one of my barters, in exchange for a returnable National Trust coat and a similarly emblazoned polo shirt and fleece, also to be handed back. The rainproof hat, a sort of upturned plant pot which makes me look like someone who became detached from a Happy Mondays gig *circa* 1990 and still hasn't found his way home, I can keep.

I phone the rangers, who are already halfway up the other side of the hill, but they agree the weather 'isn't perfect' and decide to drive over to meet me instead. We record the poem in the car, then do a second take outside for 'atmosphere', by which they mean rain, then they drive away. It's now eleven thirty and I still haven't walked a single step. I find myself thinking of the walk out of Hawes, at that stage in the journey when I was really into my stride, marching into Horton-in-Ribblesdale just after lunchtime with fourteen miles under my belt and having barely broken sweat, and now here I am just a week or so later, slacking off, letting the whole enterprise unravel. The mist and the rain hanging over the reservoir are one and the same substance, a swaying, dismal curtain, thinning occasionally, offering chinks of light, threatening even to open onto sunlight and brightness every now and again, but then closing and thickening, drawing a heavy veil over the valley and the view. Fear is what is stopping me. I don't mind the wet and the cold, but I don't want to get lost. The Cheviots were horrible, but at least I could see. Cross Fell was a nightmare, but I had company there, plus a dog, plus fell-runners waiting to reel me in. This time it's just me. For a few tantalising minutes I think about doing a Donald Crowhurst: I could just mooch around in one of the valleys for five or six hours, make a few notes in my book, then drive over to Edale, or somewhere near Edale, and no one would be any the wiser. Or I could just pack up and try again tomorrow, or the day after, or in a couple of months when there's a cast-iron guarantee of twelve hours of blue sky from dawn to dusk. No one said it had to be done on consecutive days, did they? Why the big fuss about doing it all in one go? Why don't I just go home?

The mist swirls. Wind rattles a few young birch trees next to the toilet block. Raindrops race and collide on the windscreen. It isn't easy pulling on waterproof over-trousers at the best of times and almost impossible in the front seat of a car, even in a roomy family saloon. And not easy retying my boots, hands scrabbling around down by the clutch pedal, cheek pressed against the steering wheel, or getting my elbows and fists through the sleeves, or zipping up a cagoule. And not easy leaving the vehicle, or standing in front of the pay-and-display ticket machine wondering how much to put in, what time I'll be back. Not easy to lock the car and set off.

A disused railway line runs parallel to the water's edge and the road, now used as a cycle path, and I walk along it for half a mile or so, in an odd frame of mind, head down, barging straight through a gang of half a dozen sheep and a ram who wants to stand his ground till the last moment. Straight through a few long and deep puddles I would have circumnavigated or vaulted on happier days. This isn't really the Pennine Way, which actually comes across the valley above Rhodeswood Reservoir, so I've missed out about seven or eight hundred yards of the actual trail, but I'm not in the mood for nit-picking pedantry and petty, hair-splitting rules.

I spot the sign at the gate, walking towards Reaps Farm, where a big ugly dog struts about in a mesh cage, growling and snarling. Then the path veers abruptly and unapologetically upwards, in what feels like an almost vertical ascent, heading into the nothingness of the mist. This is the mouth of Torside Clough. I'd noticed it yesterday from Laddow Rocks, and had taken a dislike to it even from that distance, being uncharacteristically severe and gloomy, even for the Peak District, infolded and secretive, with a fjord-like steepness to the scarred, striated sides and a deeply incised watercourse lurking somewhere at the bottom of its rocky channel. An abyss more than a valley, a long, narrow trench, better suited to some underwater location in the middle of the Atlantic than these moors, home to several unclassified species of sea creature with no eyes, transparent flesh and pulsing, fibre-optic veins. As well as mist, steam appears to be rising out of the gorge, and I catch occasional glimpses of what in this scenario might be tropical ferns of some kind underneath the rocks to each side. The path is stony, hard on the ankles, and where there aren't stones there are puddles of black water or patches of black mud. I keep climbing, and even though the clough is a cauldron full of cloud vapour and hanging rain, with no visible dimensions, the nausea of vertigo still washes across me, and intuitively I can sense the growing depth and the sheerness of the fall.

Out of nowhere, four apocalyptic hikers suddenly emerge, young lads carrying full packs, pots and pans swinging from their rucksacks, mud-stains right up to their waists. They look like lost and broken cowboys whose steeds have bolted during a thunderstorm. Every part of them drips or glistens with water. They splash past with a few grunts and a quick flash of recognition in their eyes, then dissolve into the mist. Twenty minutes later I pass a couple who look as if they are kitted out to withstand biological warfare or a chemical attack, in big moon boots, chunky thermal mittens, salopettes and quilted anoraks with hoods pinched tightly around their faces, their eyes hidden by goggles, their mouths covered with scarves. They appear then disappear, insulated against the outside world and inoculated against any pleasantries I might want to exchange. The path eventually seems to plateau out but it might just be an optical illusion because walking still feels like an uphill task; either way I must be nearing the head of the valley because the stream is now running adjacent to the track, and in fact IS the track every once in a while. I fish a Mars Bar out of the bag, 'fish' being an unfortunately accurate verb in this instance, then I go on.

If ever a signpost is needed on the Pennine Way it is at John Track Well, an actual water well, apparently, though I don't spot one (and certainly don't need one), because it's here that the trail suddenly crosses the stream and sets off at a right angle, bearing due east. Perhaps from the other direction the junction is impossible to miss, but by this approach it is a disaster waiting to happen, and I duly oblige, unable to imagine that such a turning would go unrecognised given the potential consequences of getting lost on Bleaklow. In other words it is not my fault that instead of making a sharp left at the ford I plough on across the moor until the stream fizzles out, and with it the path.

I believe that as a race we have certain instinctive powers, and that one of those powers is the ability to make the correct decision in almost every circumstance. This can apply to all kinds of social and emotional situations as well as to straightforward issues of navigation. But we also have an extraordinary capacity for ignoring those instincts and for convincing ourselves otherwise. Why or how we do it I don't know: maybe we've reached a state of evolutionary complacency, maybe our pig-headedness has won out over our gut feeling, or maybe we just like a bit of drama every now and again. So at some very primitive and elemental level I know that I have missed the turn, but there's nothing I can do, apart from carry on regardless. The weather is disgusting, filthy. It's rained many times before on this walk but I've never been this wet, as if I'm leaking, water getting in through all the gaps and holes. With each step my feet squelch in my boots, and my underwear feels like it needs wringing out. Holding to what seems like a steady course I find myself after what might be another hour among those weird black dunes of peat, in that eerie lunar landscape of 'hags' and 'groughs' the guide books talk about. More than anything it looks like the aftermath of a war, the First World War, the ground shelled and cratered, with little rat runs and trenches between the grass-topped hillocks and mounds, some of which are taller than me. The water percolating through and among them is liquorice-coloured, or the colour of stewed tea, edged with a frothy scum. At the base of some of the gullies, sand and yellowy grit forms a light-coloured crust, beach-like and at odds with the general monochromatic desolation.

I come to a kind of T-junction with fresh boot prints going left, from the four horseless men of the apocalypse and two weapons inspectors I passed earlier, presumably. I'm on the right track because I see a sign, then I'm walking on causey paving, though when I've calmed down enough to get the GPS out and make sense of the map through the rain-smeared case, I calculate that I've somehow managed to bypass both Bleaklow Head and the two 'kissing' Wain Stones, the only real landmarks on this stretch. The isolation up here is all-encompassing. Less than twenty miles away in several directions people are sitting in offices checking their emails and sipping their cappuccinos, but that's a world away. Up here, you might as well be on one of Jupiter's outlying moons.

*

There are dozens of different terms to describe the act of walking, but the vocabulary now entering my mind tends to come from the less exhilarating end of the spectrum. Right now I am *tramping*. It is a *trudge*. A *grind*. I *slog* along the 'drain' of Devil's Dyke, crossing Doctor's Gate, a Roman road originally but also the place where a local apothecary won back his soul from Beelzebub by leaping the dyke ahead of his forked-tailed, horny-headed, cloven-hoofed rival. I wouldn't mind doing a similar bit of bargaining at the moment, a couple of poems for a few hours of sunlight, a whole book even for just a break in the weather or a gap in the clouds, but where is Satan when you need him?

It's three thirty by the time I come splattering and spluttering onto the A57, the legendary Snake Pass so beloved by motorbike enthusiasts, day-trippers and couriers of illegal substances. Near its lower reaches sits Ladybower and other reservoirs of the Upper Derwent, home to several pairs of goshawks, the testing site for the bouncing bomb and setting for the film *The Dam Busters*. At the top, where I am, lies some of the most exposed and windswept moorland in the country, and it doesn't take much more than a few flurries of snow for the red warning lights down in the towns to start pulsing on and off, indicating that the road is closed. I enjoy the feel of tarmac on the soles of my boots for a few strides, then set off across Featherbed Moss, and miss the path again by trying a little short cut, hoping to make up lost time, then find it, then lose it once more, then slosh towards a stake in the ground, then on to the next stake and the next, until I reach what I take to be the 'flint factory' of Mill Hill, where the route turns ninety degrees from the south-west to the south-east, and where the stakes end. I'm not just wet, I'm saturated, from top to bottom and from outside to in. Waterlogged. And chilly, and shivery. I can feel my body heat leaching away through the damp, clingy fabric of my clothes and being spirited off across the landscape by the nagging wind. And through the weather there's just enough visibility to see how the path ascends to the final summit of Kinder Scout, not just into grey, drifting mist, but into real black-hearted clouds, malignant, intimidating, a nightmare to enter.

And I can't do it. I can't bring myself to walk up into that darkness on my own. Can't let go of the last wooden stake and go wading out into the deep, can't summon up the spirit of Odysseus or Sir Gawain, or invoke the determination of those mass trespassers who defied shotguns and truncheons to open up this very place to the likes of me, can't even draw strength from muleteer Robert Kirby and the weight and worth of his war medals, wrapped in a freezer bag in my shirt pocket beneath several layers of sodden fleeces and coats. Twenty years ago I tried to cross Kinder Scout from the other side and couldn't. It's as if there's some membrane of weather or wall of circumstance out there which I can never breach, no matter how I approach or attack it, either from a standing start or from an eighteen-day run-up. I'd come here today to stick two fingers up at this walk by swaggering along the home straight then refusing to cross the line. Instead, it refuses me.

I stand on Mill Hill for another half an hour, looking in different directions, thinking about the 250 miles behind me and the five or six in front, waiting for a break in the weather or some surge of courage to carry me up that hill, through the blackness and into the light on the other side. But nothing changes. Everything stays the same.

So I fail. I don't finish the Pennine Way. I turn around and go home.

Rambling On

I realised at an early stage on the walk that taking notes with pen and paper was going to be completely impractical, but I was determined to try to keep some sort of contemporaneous record of the journey, so I talked into the voice recorder on my mobile phone as I went along, then made transcriptions in the evening. On that final day, in my confused state somewhere between Bleaklow and Kinder Scout, I'd put the phone back into my top pocket but must have forgotten to turn it off. It was a couple of weeks before I got round to playing it back, but when I did, sitting on a beach in Cornwall, recuperating, it haunted me. The recording lasts for forty-eight minutes and twelve seconds, and consists mainly of splashy footsteps, the sound of rain against man-made fibres, wet 'waterproofs' chafing against themselves, and heavy breathing. In and amongst the breaths are some even heavier sighs, several unrepeatable blasphemous expletives, two rhetorical questions of a philosophical nature, and towards the end, a kind of low-level whimpering, followed by ten minutes of inexplicable inaction, with only the sound of the weather in the background, like static or white noise.

I've kept the recording. In fact I've downloaded it onto my iPod, so every now and again when I'm listening on random shuffle with headphones clamped around my ears

I'm suddenly transported back to that desolate and god-forsaken hill. What it doesn't report is that on the way back to the car that terrible evening, slithering down Torside with the rain still chasing me and the dusk not far behind, I saw a bird on the path which I thought at first was a thrush, then a large blackbird. But before flying off it turned to face me, and I saw the white bib under its throat, and realised it was a ring ouzel, something of a rarity and a bird I'd never seen before. I can't claim that it made the whole sorry and soggy day worthwhile, but it reminded me that I'd set out in search of experiences rather than conquests, and this was as welcome and as unexpected as any, a metaphorical and literal moment of brightness on an otherwise grey and grim occasion.

If the word recuperate seems a bit strong, then I apologise. After all it wasn't as if I'd just returned from a tour of duty in Afghanistan or climbed Everest without oxygen, and during the walk itself I felt fit and healthy and physically capable of making it all the way. But I suffer with a bad back, once diagnosed as ankylosing spondylitis then reclassified as far less impressive 'lower back-pain syndrome' during the late nineties. As a pre-emptive measure I started a course of pain-killers the week before I set off. I never felt any discomfort, but didn't know if that was due to the drugs or the efficacious effects of regular exercise, so carried on popping a few of the little red pills each day, just to play safe. When I'd finished the walk I threw the pills in the bin, and two days later I seized up, and needed the best part of a week in bed before I felt well enough to hobble downstairs and shuffle around the garden in a dressing gown. Had I really walked from Scotland to Derbyshire, or had I just floated along on a cushion of Diclofenac?

In many ways, the Pennine Way is a pointless exercise, leading from nowhere in particular to nowhere in particular, via no particular route, and for no particular reason. But to embark on the walk is to surrender to its lore and submit to its logic, and to take up a challenge against the self. Physically, I'd assumed I wasn't up to it, and it turned out I was. Mentally I thought I was more than equal to the task; turned out I wasn't. My other challenge was to validate myself as a travelling poet, and on the face of it, I succeeded. Over the course of nineteen days I pocketed a grand total of £3,086.42, and read poems to 1,158 people. From that sum, I can also calculate that each venue generated average gate receipts of £171.47, and that each audience member thought my performance was worth £2.66 (though given the number of tenners and even twenty-pound notes slipped into the sock each night by some kind-hearted individuals, I have to concede that a few others thought I was worth nothing). That income, though, is only half the story, because from the other pocket I shelled out for the following:

Complete set of OS maps: £76.50
Complete set of Harvey's waterproof 'detailed'
maps: £29.85
Waterproof map-case: £16.00
Guide books: £67.86
GPS system: £85.99
Compass: £19.00
Back-up compass: £19.00
Safety whistle: £2.00

2 compact aluminium poles: £51.98

Mammut Teton GTX size 10 boots: £79.99

Inner socks: £27.98

Outer socks: £60.00

Blister plasters: £4.00

Blister stick: £4.00

Compeed toe-pack: £2.00

Waterproof Gore-tex coat: £89.99

Waterproof cape: £23.00

2 pairs walking trousers: £72.00

Waterproof over-trousers: £24.99

Fleece: £19.99

Gloves: £17.99

Hat: £1.00

Batteries: £14.99

Single train ticket to Berwick-upon-Tweed: £56.10

Accommodation where not provided: £80.00

Meals/drinks where not provided: £72.86

Alcohol where not provided: £52.65

Mobile-phone bill: £33.81

Tips/bribes/bungs: £40.00

All other extras: £29.29

A total of £1,174.81, leaving a net profit of £1,911.61. Still not bad for just less than three weeks' work, though most days began at eight in the morning and ended at ten at night, which by my calculation implies an overall hourly rate of £7.19, not exactly a fat-cat salary with an investment banker's bonus. In fact only £1.11 above the minimum wage. Of course it's true that I had a better time than I would have if I'd been flipping burgers or picking turnips all summer, yet as a career move, it suggests that taking to the road on a permanent basis would be a bad idea. For one thing I'd probably drop dead after about three months, fulfilling my father's prophecy of being found in a ditch dressed only in a wind-shredded refuse sack. And for another, reading poems isn't like doing a milk-round or delivering papers, where services and supplies are provided to the same customers around the same circuit over and over again. To keep selling my wares I'd have to stray further and further afield in search of new audiences, becoming more of a stranger every day, both at home and abroad. Neither does the raw economic data take into account the unquantifiable acts of goodwill and thoughtfulness that came my way during the walk from kind and generous people, gifts of time, effort, experience and expense, without which I wouldn't have been able even to begin the Pennine Way, let alone complete it (OK, almost complete it). I was made welcome wherever I travelled, never once going without food, shelter, company, or somewhere to rest my head, and maybe it's on those terms alone that I should judge this undertaking and ask to be judged, because for anyone setting out on an adventure in poetry, be it a long walk or an entire career, could any more validation be expected or hoped for?

Finally, the question a lot of people have asked me since I came home: would I walk the Pennine Way again? My answer: no. Well, maybe, but if I did, I'd rely more on my feet next time and less on my tongue; take fewer poems with me, and hopefully bring a few more back. And I'd take someone brave and intrepid with me, someone not daunted by mist or intimidated by dark clouds, to guide me across the Cheviots, to hold my hand over Cross Fell, and to part the black curtain which hangs over Kinder Scout and lead me through.

Cotton Grass

Hand-maidens, humble courtiers,
yes-men in silver wigs,
they stoop low at the path's edge, bow
to the military parade
of boot and stick.

Then it's back to the work,
to the acid acres.
To wade barefoot through waterlogged peat,
trawling the breeze, carding the air
for threads of sheep-wool snagged on the breeze.

Letting time blaze through their ageless hair
like the wind.

Credit Where Credit Is Due

Thanks first and foremost are due to friend and fellow poet Caroline Hawkridge. At a very early stage in the project I realised I didn't have anything like the organisational skills to make this walk happen, and without either laughing or fainting, she responded to my plea for help with such enthusiasm, optimism and managerial panache that I now shudder to think how things might have turned out without her assistance. In the planning stages she fielded enquiries, nobbled unsuspecting locals, tracked down possible contacts and moulded offers of help into a workable itinerary. During the actual walk she operated a kind of hotline-switchboard from a field position somewhere in Cheshire, and developed such a rapport with so many individuals along the Pennine Way I think they were slightly disappointed when I turned up rather than her. And all this at a time in her life when she had better things to do, so my gratitude is total.

In rough chronological order I would also like to express my sincere thanks to the following, for their kindness and encouragement, for their time and energy, but mostly for their company, which saw me from beginning to end and transformed the Pennine Way from a walk into a journey: Al Pattullo and his wife Judith; Bridget Khursheed; Jacquie Wright, Executive Manager, Abbotsford Trust; Beverley

Rutherford, Events and Campaign Co-ordinator, Abbotsford Trust; the Borders Writers' Forum; Catherine Ross and John Wylie; poet Katrina Porteous; Steve Westwood, National Trail Officer, Natural England; Mel Whewell, member of Northumberland National Park Authority; Jonathan Manning, Editor of *Country Walking*; Tim Dee and Claire Spottiswoode; inevitable Huddersfielder Nick Batty; Frances Whitehead, Communications Officer, Northumberland National Park and the Park Rangers; Gareth and Jane Latcham at the Rose and Thistle Inn; Sarah Moor; Joyce and Colin Taylor at Forest View Walkers' Accommodation; poet Matt Bryden, Camilla and 'deer-hunter' Jess; William Morrison-Bell of Highgreen Arts and friends and family and dogs; the Bellingham Heritage Centre committee, particularly Seán MacNialluis; Dick Shevlin and family; musicians Jessica and Martha Carr, Don Clegg, Gwennie Fraser, Stephen Fry and David McCracken; Mick Blood, Manager, Once Brewed Youth Hostel; Des Garrahan; Alison Blair, Manager, Northumberland National Park Visitor Centre at Once Brewed; Wendy Bond; Sue and Dave at the Greenhead Hotel; Jane Brantom at the Hadrian Arts Trust; Danny Johnson; poet Josephine Dickinson; Mary and David Livesey at Yew Tree Chapel B&B; David Godwin; Janette Thorley and Mike and their golden retriever; Jules Cadie; Garrigill Village Hall and the Save the George and Dragon committee; Richard Brown and his dog and his friends; fell-runners Claire 'Freckle' Appleton, Hester Cox, Alastair Dunn and Andrew Calcott plus dogs plus Neil Wootton and the Fell Poets' Society; poet and Scaremonger Martin Malone; Annie Kindleysides and Brian at Meaburn Hill

Farmhouse B&B; Rick Abell; fair-weather Brian; Chris Woodley-Stewart, Director, North Pennines AONB Partnership; Shane Harris, Sustainable Tourism and Communications Officer, North Pennines AONB Partnership, and his wife Cath; Sue Matthews at Langdon Beck Hotel; J. E. & V. Winter's of Middleton-in-Teesdale; Jan Arger, General Manager, Blackton Grange; Peter Murray and Jane Hilton; alleged journalist Paul Croughton; Ben and Delphine Ruston; Vaughn Curtis, Chief Executive, the Georgian Theatre Royal in Richmond, plus colleagues Emma Vallance and Angelique; Graham Oakes; Colin Chick, Pennine Way Ranger for the Yorkshire Dales National Park; Ann Pilling and Joe and friends; Veronica Caperon; Andrew Forster at the Wordsworth Trust; Andrew 'Slug' Slegg; Adrian Pickles, Director, Malham Tarn Field Centre and his wife Jacqueline and dog Maggie; Kirsten and Chris and friends; Carey Davies, Assistant Editor of *The Great Outdoors* and Jim Morrison lookalike; Professor Glyn Turton and family; Gargrave Civic Society; Rob Hawley; Charles, kind supplier of eco-wear; Anna Turner at the Elmet Trust with her husband barefoot Johnny and Bet the dog; Rachel Connor and Rebecca Evans at the Arvon Foundation, Lumb Bank; the Ted Hughes Theatre at Calder High School; Ruth and Donald Crossley; Jeni Wetton; Jo Abell; the Armitage tribe; Subhadassi; Benjamin Judge, Rod Lyon and his son Jack and the Blackstone Edge Butty Ambushers (sorry I missed you!); Alison Mills at the National Trust's Marsden Moor Estate and James Dean at Standedge Visitor Centre (British Waterways); Martyn Sharp, Pennine Way Ranger, Peak District National Park; Lisa and Sean Caldwell; Michael

Constantine; Bay Tree Books and the Oakwood pub in Glossop; Chris Strogen; Stephanie Hinde, National Trust High Peak and Longshaw; and those countless others for their behind-the-scenes help or those whose generous offers and invitations fell beyond my schedule. And most of all to Sue, who I walked home to.

Also by SIMON ARMITAGE

ff

SIR GAWAIN AND THE GREEN KNIGHT

Preserved on a single surviving manuscript dating from around 1400, composed by an anonymous master, *Sir Gawain and the Green Knight* was rediscovered only 200 years ago, and published for the first time in 1839. One of the earliest great stories of English literature, after *Beowulf*, the poem narrates the strange tale of a green knight on a green horse, who rudely interrupts the Round Table festivities one Yuletide, casting a pall of unease over the company and challenging one of their number to a wager. The virtuous Gawain accepts, and decapitates the intruder with his own axe. Gushing blood, the knight reclaims his head, orders Gawain to seek him out a year hence, and departs. Next Yuletide Gawain dutifully sets forth ... His quest for the Green Knight involves a winter journey, a seduction scene in a dream-like castle, a dire challenge answered – and a drama of enigmatic reward disguised as psychic undoing.

'It might even be the best translation of any poem I've ever seen ... [Armitage] was put on the planet to translate this poem.' *Guardian*

'Simon Armitage's superb new translation of the poem dispels the difficulties of the Middle English while preserving the strange magic of this Arthurian tale.' *Daily Telegraph*

ff

SEEING STARS

Seeing Stars is by turns a voice and a chorus: a hyper-vivid array of dramatic monologues, allegories, parables and tall tales. Here comes everybody: Snoobie and Carla, Lippincott, Wittmann, Yoshioka, Bambuck, Dr Amsterdam, Preminger. The man whose wife drapes a border-curtain across the middle of the marital home; the English astronaut with a terrestrial outlook on life; an orgiastic cast of unreconstructed pie-worshipers at a Northern sculpture farm; the soap-opera supremacists at their zoo-wedding; the driver who picks up hitchhikers as he hurtles towards a head-on collision with Thatcherism; a Christian cheese-shop proprietor in the wrong part of town; the black bear with a dark secret, the woman who curates giant snowballs in the chest freezer. Celebrities and nobodies, all come to the ball.

'To say these poems resist classification is an understatement: they are wonderful, exuberant, unsettling entertainments that exist on their own terms. [Armitage's] voice – and its unsubdued wit – is unique.' *Observer*

'Armitage's talent for observational prose has so far seemed a second job to his poems. *Seeing Stars*, his eighth full collection, merges the two in a way that is genuinely new in British poetry . . . As an experiment with an established voice, and a strange dream of 21st-century Britain, *Seeing Stars* is a triumph, and one of my books of the year.' *Daily Telegraph*

ff

Faber and Faber is one of the great independent publishing houses. We were established in 1929 by Geoffrey Faber with T. S. Eliot as one of our first editors. We are proud to publish award-winning fiction and non-fiction, as well as an unrivalled list of poets and playwrights. Among our list of writers we have five Booker Prize winners and twelve Nobel Laureates, and we continue to seek out the most exciting and innovative writers at work today.

Find out more about our authors and books
faber.co.uk

Read our blog for insight and opinion on books and the arts
thethoughtfox.co.uk

Follow news and conversation
twitter.com/faberbooks

Watch readings and interviews
youtube.com/faberandfaber

Connect with other readers
facebook.com/faberandfaber

Explore our archive
flickr.com/faberandfaber